W9-AZX-503

Beyond Subjective Morality

Beyond Subjective Morality

Ethical Reasoning and
Political Philosophy

JAMES S. FISHKIN

Yale University Press
New Haven and London

Published with assistance from the
foundation established in memory of
Philip Hamilton McMillan of the
Class of 1894, Yale College.

Copyright © 1984 by Yale University.
All rights reserved.
This book may not be reproduced, in whole
or in part, in any form (beyond that
copying permitted by Sections 107 and 108
of the U.S. Copyright Law and except by
reviewers for the public press), without
written permission from the publishers.

Designed by James J. Johnson
and set in Aster roman type.
Printed in the United States of America by
Vail-Ballou Press, Binghamton, New York

Library of Congress Cataloging in Publication Data

Fishkin, James S.
   Beyond subjective morality

   Includes index.
   1. Ethics. 2. Ethical relativism. 3. Moral
development. 4. Political science I. Title.
BJ1012.F538   1984   170   83 – 14701
ISBN 0–300–03048–7
        0–300–03625–6

11   10   9   8   7   6   5   4   3   2

Contents

Acknowledgments

This book began life as an empirical study. I would especially like to thank Robert E. Lane, who supervised an early dissertation version with great insight and sensitivity. I would also like to thank Kenneth Keniston and Catharine MacKinnon, my collaborators on some related empirical work.

I am especially grateful to Lawrence Kohlberg for discussions of both his work and mine over the past decade. Only someone as morally developed as Larry Kohlberg would have been as generous with a critic as he has been with me.

Eventually the philosophical issues came to dominate my thinking on moral development. Interviews are employed in this book merely as illustrations, and the argument is now primarily theoretical. For discussions that contributed directly to the argument here I am grateful to Bernard Williams, Bruce Ackerman, Brian Barry, Douglas Rae, Robert Dahl, David Braybrooke, and Charles Anderson. I would also like to thank Milton Fisher, Ed Lindblom, Ian Robertson, Owen Fiss, Carol Gilligan, Heinrich von Staden, and Marie Rogers. Beverly Apothaker deserves special thanks for deciphering and typing several illegible versions of the manuscript.

My wife, Shelley, lived with this project—and its author's changing fields—as much as I did. She deserves more credit for the result than I can acknowledge here.

1. Ethical Reasoning and Moral Development

1.1. Introduction

What basis is there for moral principles? How, if at all, can they be established or justified? Such questions are *meta-ethical*: they probe the very foundations of morality.

Meta-ethics has been treated, within universities, as a comparatively obscure appendage of moral philosophy. However, it is also a subject that we all must face, if we are to have ethical convictions worthy of the name—convictions that can survive active questioning rather than convictions that have merely been passively received.

One novelty of this book is that I will explore some of the ways in which ordinary moral reasoners—nonprofessional philosophers—grapple with meta-ethical questions in arriving at their own philosophical positions, their own most cherished convictions on the great questions of life. Many ordinary reasoners, when confronted with meta-ethical problems, feel constrained by the logic of their questioning to adopt extremely skeptical positions. They feel constrained to answer meta-ethical questions in the negative, concluding that they have no adequate basis for adopting one moral view rather than another. The choice among competing values comes to be seen as arbitrary, as a matter of mere taste or preference, as a matter of purely personal subjectivity.

In this book I will probe the logic underlying this subjective view of morality in the forms that constitute a common part of our contemporary moral culture, that is, in the forms that occur among ordinary reasoners. My intention is philosophical—to demonstrate that the arguments trapping ordinary reasoners in subjectivism need not be inescapable. I will do this by showing how assumptions crucial to their reasoning (assumptions that are familiar elements of our common moral culture) can be discarded.

But this philosophical response to the arguments of ordinary reasoners will not be aimed at erecting new certainties. Meta-ethical questions, I will argue, are inevitably controversial, and the foundations of morality are unavoidably open to reasonable disagreement. Despite this inconclusiveness, my object will be to free us from constraining assumptions that wrongly appear to render subjectivism the only viable position, the only viable interpretation of the controversiality that does inevitably apply to the foundations of morality.

My arguments for the avoidability of subjectivism have implications for political theory and in particular for liberalism. Independent of particular religious and metaphysical assumptions—assumptions among which a modern liberal state must presumably maintain a certain neutrality—can there be a nonarbitrary basis for making moral judgments? Without a positive answer to this question, liberalism must self-destruct as a coherent moral ideology. The viability of liberalism as a political theory is closely tied to the possibility of a secular moral culture founded on something other than the controversial religious or metaphysical assumptions of any particular group. If, in order to maintain neutrality among religious and metaphysical assumptions, a liberal state must be constrained from any rational basis for values at all, then its foundational assumptions are *self-delegitimating*, that is, they undermine their own moral legitimacy by entailing the arbitrariness, the sheer subjectivity, of all moral claims, including any claims that can be made on behalf of the liberal state itself.

I will argue that liberal theory can be protected from this kind of foundational crisis. But protecting it requires a substantial revision of moral assumptions that have a prominent place in our culture. In proposing this revision, my aim will be to insulate both liberal theory and individual morality from the constraining assumptions that otherwise trap both in subjectivism. In doing so, I hope to develop the second chief novelty in this book—an exploration into some of the main connections between meta-ethics and political philosophy.[1] However, before connecting the discussion explicitly to political theory, let us begin with the empirical study of moral reasoning.

1.2. Subjectivism and Kohlberg's Theory

For the last two decades the dominant paradigm in the empirical study of moral reasoning has been the theory of "moral development" originated by Lawrence Kohlberg. Building on the cognitive-developmental work of Jean Piaget, Kohlberg began with a study of seventy-five Chicago boys interviewed at three intervals from early adolescence (ages 10–16) into adulthood (ages 22–28). He found that his subjects progressed through stages in a definite sequence. While some progressed through the entire sequence, others stabilized at some point along the way. This initial study was supplemented by studies of other cultures that found the same fundamental sequence of stages and by studies connecting moral judgment to action and to other forms of cognitive activity.[2]

1. Some connections between meta-ethics and political philosophy are also explored in quite different ways in other recent work. See Thomas Landon Thorson, *The Logic of Democracy* (New York: Holt, Rinehart and Winston, 1962); Roberto Mangabeira Unger, *Knowledge and Politics* (New York: The Free Press, 1975); and Thomas A. Spragens, *The Irony of Liberal Reason* (Chicago: University of Chicago Press, 1981).

2. For a systematic overview see Lawrence Kohlberg, "From Is to Ought: How to Commit the Naturalistic Fallacy and Get Away with It in the Study of Moral Development," in T. Mischel, ed., *Cognitive Development and Epistemology* (New York: Academic Press, 1971), pp. 151–235. For a wide-ranging methodological critique of some of these claims see William Kurtines and Esther Blank

CHART 1   Summary of Kohlberg's Stages of
Moral Development*

Levels	*Stages of Development*
I. Preconventional level: Moral value resides in external, quasi-physical happenings, in bad acts, or in quasi-physical needs rather than in persons and standards.	Stage 1: Obedience and punishment orientation. Stage 2: Naively egoistic orientation.
II. Conventional level: Moral value resides in performing good or right roles, in maintaining the conventional order and the expectancies of others.	Stage 3: Good-boy orientation. Conformity to stereotypical images of role behavior. Stage 4: Authority and social order maintaining orientation.
III. Postconventional level: Moral value resides in conformity by the self to shared or shareable standards, rights, and duties.	Stage 5: Contractual legalistic orientation. Stage 6: Conscience or principle orientation.

*Adapted, in abbreviated form, from Lawrence Kohlberg, "Education for Justice," in *Moral Education*, ed. T. Sizer (Cambridge, Mass.: Harvard University Press, 1970): 71–72.

Kohlberg's six stages are briefly summarized in chart 1. The great majority of moral reasoners, according to Kohlberg,

---

Grief, "The Development of Moral Thought: Review and Evaluation of Kohlberg's Approach," *Psychological Bulletin* 81, no. 8 (August 1974): 453–70. Their two most important conclusions are that the evidence for invariant sequence—particularly beyond the first three stages—is inconclusive and that there is more "regression," that is, subjectivism, than Kohlberg had admitted (before he abandoned the "regression" hypothesis in favor of the "transitional" one). They also make useful criticisms of the way in which the Kohlberg dilemmas have never progress beyond the middle "conventional level" defined by stages 3 and 4. The question of what is morally appropriate is settled for them by stereotypes of virtue (acting as a "good person" would in a given situation) or by the acknowledged rules of society (acting as "law and order" would dictate).[3]

However, Kohlberg's findings were thrown into disarray by the discovery of large numbers of subjective moral reasoners (termed relativists by the Kohlberg researchers). Consider some examples of how they evade Kohlberg's classifications in responding to one of his moral dilemmas. I will refer to the following story as the "Heinz dilemma":

> In Europe, a woman was near death from a very bad disease, a special kind of cancer. There was one drug that the doctors thought might save her. It was a form of radium that a druggist in the same town had recently discovered. The drug was expensive to make, but the druggist was charging ten times what the drug cost him to make it. He paid $200 for the radium and charged $2000 for a small dose of the drug. The sick woman's husband, Heinz, went to everyone he knew to borrow the money, but he could only get together about $1,000, which is half of what it cost. He told the druggist that his wife was dying, and asked him to sell it cheaper or let him pay later. But the druggist said, "No, I discovered the drug and I'm going to make money from it." So Heinz got desperate and broke into the man's store to steal the drug for his wife. Should Heinz have done that? Was it actually wrong or right? Why?[4]

One of the earliest subjectivists cited by Kohlberg is Roger, age 20, who surfaced in a study of the Berkeley Free Speech

---

sometimes been administered and scored. See appendix A for further discussion of regression and transition within Kohlberg's theory.

3. See Kohlberg, "From Is to Ought," pp. 163–80. Kohlberg also cites opinion poll data supporting his conclusion that the American population is overwhelmingly "conventional." For example, about three quarters responded to the Heinz dilemma (dilemma 1, appendix D) by saying that it would be morally wrong for Heinz to steal the drug to save his wife's life, although many admitted they might do so. See Lawrence Kohlberg, "Indoctrination versus Relativity in Value Education," *Zygon* 6 (1971): 285–310, especially 291–92.

4. Kohlberg, "From Is to Ought," p. 156.

Movement. Roger responds to the Heinz dilemma by insisting on the purely "subjective" nature of any judgment he might make about Heinz's action of stealing the drug to save his wife's life. Heinz, he says, "was a victim of circumstances and can only be judged by other men whose varying values and interest frameworks produce subjective decisions which are neither permanent nor absolute."

Was it Heinz's duty to save his wife's life? It is not up to Roger to determine. "A husband's duty is up to the husband to decide," he says, "and anybody can judge him, and he can judge anybody's judgment. If he values her life over the consequences of theft," Roger concludes, "he should do it."

Does the druggist have a right to charge as much as he wants? Roger is equally adept at avoiding this question. "One can talk about rights until doomsday and never say anything." He asks, "Does the lion have a right to the zebra's life when he starves? When he wants sport? Or when he will take it at will? Does he consider rights? Is man so different?"[5]

Another subjectivist cited by Kohlberg (an advanced high school student named Bob) was willing to excuse Heinz but implied that he was also willing to excuse the druggist—provided that the latter was conforming to his own "capitalist morality":

> There's a million ways to look at it. Heinz had a moral decision to make. Was it worse to steal or to let his wife die? In my mind I can either condemn him or condone him. In this case I think it was fine. But possibly the druggist was working on a capitalist morality of supply and demand.

Kohlberg went on to ask Bob, "Would it be wrong if he did not steal it?"

5. Ibid., p. 180. The Kohlberg researchers refer to these cases as "relativists." I will refer to them as subjectivists in order to conform to the distinctions refined in chapter 2.

It depends on how he is oriented morally. If he thinks it's worse to steal than to let his wife die, then it would be wrong what he did. It's all relative, what I would do is steal the drug. I can't say that's right or wrong or that's what everyone should do.[6]

It is difficult to fit these subjectivists within the Kohlberg scheme. At first they were interpreted as having retrogressed from stage 4 or 5 to the childlike reasoning of instrumental hedonism (stage 2). But such an interpretation would violate the basic assumption of the theory that people progress through the stages in a single invariant sequence. A more recent strategy has been to interpret subjectivism as a transitional phenomenon between stages 4 and 5, a stage 4 1/2, if you will. However, this transitional phenomenon between stages has in many cases enough stability to be interpreted as a stage in its own right. Furthermore, there is no evidence that it is reliably followed by stage 5. Little justification exists for treating it as part of the transition to stage 5 unless it is actually followed by stage 5. For a detailed discussion of the difficulties posed by subjectivism for Kohlberg's theory see appendix A. I will offer a fresh start here based on classifications of a different kind.

Subjectivism poses a basic challenge to the Kohlberg scheme because it is essentially a meta-ethical phenomenon, while Kohlberg's classifications are normative ethical. Normative ethics offers particular prescriptions for action or general principles that imply particular prescriptions in situations of moral choice. Subjectivist reasoners, by contrast, question their basis for making any moral judgments at all. They are taking a general meta-ethical position about the basic structure and ultimate legitimacy of morality.[7] This position cannot be

6. Lawrence Kohlberg and Carol Gilligan, "The Adolescent as a Philosopher: The Discovery of the Self in a Post-Conventional World," *Daedalus* 100 (1971): 1073.

7. The distinction between normative ethics and meta-ethics is a standard one. See, for example, William K. Frankena, *Ethics* (Englewood Cliffs:

squeezed into any particular niche in Kohlberg's sequence of normative ethical stages.

Once the meta-ethical character of subjectivism is realized, it can be seen as a *resolution* to perplexities rather than as a source of them. In other words, the same motivation for consistency and equilibrium which, according to Kohlberg, drives reasoners through his sequence of stages, also drives some of them instead to subjectivism. These reasoners are deflected in this way because of the logic of a pattern of questioning that renders subjectivism uniquely attractive as an alternative.

Of course, normative ethical and meta-ethical reasoning are commonly intermixed. In fact, I uncovered the meta-ethical arguments discussed here simply by probing the responses given to some normative ethical questions, in Kohlberg's moral dilemmas and other dilemmas of a similar kind. But the distinction is important to my claim that subjectivism has been misunderstood. For what may appear in normative ethical terms as sheer confusion may in meta-ethical terms be an attempt to arrive at a consistent and intellectually defensible position.[8]

From this perspective, it should not be surprising that those who question what Kohlberg calls conventional morality should find themselves confronting subjectivism. For once a conventional basis for one's values is brought into question, a problem obviously arises: how are those values to be supported or justified? This is the essential *meta-ethical* question. To understand how reasoners grapple with it requires an analysis of the arguments that underlie substantive positions rather than an analysis of substantive positions themselves.

Once the psychological phenomenon of meta-ethical questioning is properly identified, a philosophical issue naturally presents itself. If, as I shall argue, ordinary reasoners arrive at

---

Prentice-Hall, 1963), p. 4, and Richard B. Brandt, *Ethical Theory* (Englewood Cliffs: Prentice-Hall, 1959), pp. 4–7.

8. For charges of inconsistency and confusion directed at subjectivism see Kohlberg, "From Is to Ought," p. 179, and Elliot Turiel, "Conflict and Transition in Adolescent Moral Development," *Child Development* 45, no. 1 (1974): 14–29.

one form or another of subjectivism because they regard it as *more* consistent and defensible than the alternatives, how adequate are the arguments that impel them to this conclusion? If, as I shall claim, the key arguments they characteristically employ constitute valid inferences, given their assumptions, how reasonable are those assumptions?

Since these reasoners offer powerful arguments from widely shared assumptions, their subjectivism constitutes a basic challenge to the viability of our common moral culture. They make a powerful case that, from widely shared premises, the conclusion is inescapable that our common value judgments are fundamentally arbitrary, no more than a matter of personal taste. This book offers a response to that challenge by demonstrating how certain of their crucial assumptions can be discarded. As we shall see, the force of their arguments can be admitted, yet it is possible for us to withstand the seemingly irresistible pressure toward subjectivism. How that can be accomplished will depend upon the scheme of meta-ethical positions introduced next.

2. Seven Ethical Positions

2.1. A Scheme of Classification

Thus far I have spoken generally of subjective ethical positions. The Kohlberg researchers have used a similar general category ("relativism"). But subjective reasoners may be distinguished in important ways. Some say they must refrain from making any moral judgments at all. Others, by contrast, believe they can make moral judgments—but of themselves and not of others. There are also relativists who judge others—but in terms of their own respective values. In addition, some subjective reasoners apply their own values universally to everyone—but maintain, nevertheless, that those values are only arbitrary personal tastes.

In this chapter I will introduce seven ethical positions. Four will be variations of subjectivism that distinguish the positions just cited—positions that I have thus far treated together under the general heading of subjectivism. The remaining three positions in the scheme take the contrasting, objective view: they regard at least some moral judgments as justified or rationally supportable.

I believe that the seven positions defined by the total scheme combine to capture the full range of possible consistent positions on the issues that they classify. In other words, the subjective and objective positions together exhaust the consistent possibilities. While further subdivisions are, of course, possible, this scheme exhausts the consistent possibilities in the sense that any consistent position on the issues classified by the scheme must fit one, and only one, of the proposed seven possibilities.

The strongest claim commonly made on behalf of a moral position is:

> *Claim 1:* One's judgments are *absolute*, that is, their inviolable character is rationally unquestionable.

By "inviolable" judgments I mean those formulated in terms of principles that it would always be wrong[1] to violate. One is never morally justified, in other words, in overruling such absolute principles. In addition to being inviolable, an absolute judgment is also "rationally unquestionable," by which I mean that it is not open to reasonable disagreement. Perhaps it is a necessary truth, if such a thing is possible in ethical matters. Or if it is not a necessary truth, it has a kind of apodeictic basis that renders further skepticism inappropriate. Of course, any particular position that laid claim to this characteristic would have to include a further account of the meaning of "rational" or "reasonable" and of the basis for the principle's immunity from reasonable questioning. But such details of particular positions need not concern us at the moment.

A second, less demanding claim would weaken the absolutist character of the basis attributed to one's judgments. Let us identify it as:

> *Claim 2:* One's judgments are *inviolable*, that is, it would be objectively wrong ever to violate (permit exceptions to) them.

---

1. Such a principle is strong rather than weak or prima facie. For further discussion of this distinction and related issues see James Fishkin, *The Limits of Obligation* (New Haven and London: Yale University Press, 1982), chap. 6. Violating such a strong principle, even when it conflicts with another, is wrong or morally prohibited. Conflicts among principles of this kind are often dramatized by tragic situations. See Bernard Williams, *Problems of the Self* (Cambridge: Cambridge University Press, 1977), pp. 172–74.

According to claim 2, one may attribute an "objective" basis to judgments that hold without exception. However, the objective basis, which we still need to clarify, falls short of the absolutist claim that a judgment is rationally unquestionable (claim 1).

A third, even less demanding claim may be identified as:

Claim 3: One's judgments are *objectively valid,* that is, their consistent application to everyone is supported by considerations that anyone should accept, were he to view the problem from what is contended to be the appropriate moral perspective.

This claim no longer includes the inviolability requirement. Such judgments may be formulated as weak, prima facie, or "ceteris paribus" principles that may, with logical consistency, be overridden in cases of conflict with other principles. Furthermore, unlike the absolute and inviolable judgments discussed above, they need not take the form of general principles at all. They may be formulated merely as particular judgments applied to specific cases.

But such judgments, even though not inviolable, fall under a minimal claim of objective validity (as do principles conforming to claim 2 above). The proponent of such a moral judgment claims that from the appropriate moral perspective, one that he believes should have jurisdiction over anyone's choice of values (one that, in other words, he believes to be valid for anyone), there is support sufficient for the adoption of his position.[2] This notion of the "appropriate moral perspective" may be formalized in a moral decision procedure such as Rawls's original position or the perfectly sympathetic spectator of the classical utilitarians. We shall explore such decision procedures below, in chapter 4. Or it may be simply the informal appeal to impartiality familiar from the Golden Rule or from

---

2. The notion of "objective" moral judgments in definitions 2 and 3 above is the same. The difference between the two claims is in the permissibility of exceptions or overridings. They are compatible with claim 3 but not with claim 2.

appeals that one should look at a situation from the perspective of the others affected. As Thomas Nagel characterizes it, "The general form of moral reasoning is to put yourself in other people's shoes."[3] However formal or informal, such notions of the moral point of view—of the appropriate impartial perspective for making moral judgments—provide the basis for a claim that a given moral position has objective validity. Of course, proponents of different positions may have quite different notions of the appropriate moral perspective from which values ought to be derived or chosen; but that is only another way of saying that the objective validity claim (3, above) is far weaker than the absolutist claim (1, above). It is weaker because it does not claim that the basis for the judgment is beyond reasonable question. Unlike claim 1, no immunity from rational disagreement is claimed for the crucial assumptions, the "appropriate moral perspective" from which the judgment can be supported.[4]

A fourth, even weaker claim may be defined as:

Claim 4: One's judgments apply *universalizably*, that is, they apply consistently to everyone, so that relevantly similar cases are treated similarly.

If a moral judgment is formulated as a general principle such as "All avoidable killing of human beings is forbidden," then the meaning of its universalizable application is evident from the definition. However, if a moral judgment is formulated merely for a particular case, such as "X should not have murdered Y on September 22," then so long as the applicability of similar judgments to relevantly similar cases is granted, the universalizability claim is satisfied. I will not interpret this claim as requiring that the criteria for relevantly similar cases

3. Thomas Nagel, *Mortal Questions* (Cambridge: Cambridge University Press, 1979), p. 126.

4. See the discussion of reflective equilibrium below. The first three claims in this scheme are briefly discussed in chapter 5 of James Fishkin, *Justice, Equal Opportunity, and the Family* (New Haven and London: Yale University Press, 1983).

be spelled out, so long as the application of the judgment to such cases is granted. One could not, in other words, grant that the murder of B by A was like the murder of Y by X in all relevant respects and then condone the former while also condemning the latter.[5]

A fifth, even weaker claim may be defined as:

Claim 5: One's judgments apply *interpersonally*, that is, to others as well as to oneself.

This claim is weaker than universalizability because one may apply moral judgments interpersonally without applying them universalizably, that is, consistently to everyone. For example, a relativist may attempt to deal with moral disagreements by applying X's values to X and Y's values to Y. Such a relativist still makes judgments of others, but he refrains from applying the values involved with universalizable consistency: X's values, for example, are not applied to relevantly similar cases involving Y, and Y's values are not applied to relevantly similar cases involving X.

Last, the weakest of the claims is:

Claim 6: One's judgments apply to oneself.

As we shall see, some subjective reasoners deal with issues of moral disagreement by asserting this claim but none of the others, even the weak claim of interpersonal judgment. However, in avoiding even interpersonal judgment and universalizability they face questions about the sense in which their values can be recognizable as moral values and not imply at least some moral judgments of others for some possible cases. However, I will postpone discussion of these issues until later. As defined, the properties mentioned in these six claims stand in certain logical relations to one another. An absolute judgment (in the

5. I take this notion of "universalizability" from Hare's famous discussion. See R. M. Hare, *Freedom and Reason* (Oxford: Oxford University Press, 1963). For some crucial ambiguities in Hare's discussion see J. L. Mackie, *Ethics: Inventing Right and Wrong* (New York: Penguin, 1977), chap. 4.

sense of claim 1) must also be inviolable (in the sense of claim 2); it must be objectively valid (as in claim 3); it must hold with universalizable consistency (claim 4); and, obviously, it must satisfy interpersonal judgment (claim 5) and judgment of self (claim 6). These claims are defined in such a way that a moral position satisfying a given claim must, if it is to be consistent, satisfy all those *following* it in the order presented here. That is why I have presented the strongest claim first; those following it are progressively weaker. On the other hand, if a position fails to satisfy a given claim, then it must also fail to satisfy those *preceding* it, but not those following it, if it is to be consistent. For example, if a judgment is not objectively valid (claim 3), then it cannot be either inviolable (claim 2) or absolute (claim 1), according to the definitions presented here. In general, satisfaction of a claim requires satisfaction of those following it and rejection of a claim requires rejection of those preceding it—if the resulting positions are to be consistent.

Either of these two logical patterns would be sufficient to reduce the consistent possibilities for combining these claims to the seven positions depicted in chart 2. See appendix C for further discussion of these logical relations.

Accepting all six claims produces a position commonly termed *absolutism* (position I)—an assertion of rationally unquestionable principles that hold inviolably, with objective validity, with universalizability, and, of course, that apply to others as well as to oneself. Kant offers an influential philosophical illustration of this position. In accepting the necessity of moral imperatives that are "categorical," he endowed them with an "unconditional" and "apodeictic" character; as a result, they hold "let the consequences be what they may." Like all a priori judgments, they hold "with strict universality, that is, in such a manner that no exception is allowed as possible."[6]

6. The quotation is from Immanuel Kant, *Critique of Pure Reason*, translated by Norman Kemp Smith (London: Macmillan, 1929), p. 44. See also his *Groundwork of the Metaphysics of Morals*, translated by H. J. Paton (New York: Harper and Row, 1964). Kant's reluctance to permit exceptions is notorious.

CHART 2   A Scheme of Ethical Positions

	I Absolutism	II Rigorism	III Minimal Objectivism	IV Subjective Universalism	V Relativism	VI Personalism	VII Amoralism
1. The Absolutist Claim	+	−	−	−	−	−	−
2. The Inviolability Claim	+	+	−	−	−	−	−
3. The Objective Validity Claim	+	+	+	−	−	−	−
4. The Universalizability Claim	+	+	+	+	−	−	−
5. The Interpersonal Judgment Claim	+	+	+	+	+	−	−
6. The Judgment of Self Claim	+	+	+	+	+	+	−

Rejecting the absolutist claim, one may consistently embrace the five that follow, producing a position I have labeled *rigorism* (position II) because of its claim to apply objective principles rigorously, or without any exceptions.[7] Utilitarianism, on the one hand, and Rawls's theory of justice, on the other, both provide examples of such a position.[8]

If we reject both claims 1 and 2 but accept the remaining four, we find ourselves in position III, which I have labeled *minimal objectivism*. This is the weakest of the three objectivist positions (the three positions that accept objective validity). Moral principles at this position may permit exceptions and are not beyond reasonable question. In fact, judgments at this position need not be formulated in terms of general moral principles at all; they may be restricted merely to particular prescriptions for particular cases. The doctrine Rawls is most concerned to argue against, "intuitionism," offers a good example of this position. Lacking some single inviolable principle (or list of inviolable principles in lexical order), we may, nevertheless, lay claim to objective principles that are weak or prima facie, that hold only ceteris paribus and hence are capable of being overridden or traded off, one for another. Such a position is often termed *intuitionism* because it requires a careful weighing of moral factors in each particular case.[9] Isaiah Berlin's advocacy

---

For the case of lies see his "On a Supposed Right to Tell Lies from Benevolent Motives," in *The Critique of Practical Reason and Other Writings in Moral Philosophy*, edited and translated by Lewis White Beck (Chicago: University of Chicago Press, 1949).

7. I take the term *rigorism* from Marcus George Singer, who employs it for the notion that "certain moral values hold absolutely or in all circumstances" (*Generalization in Ethics* [New York: Atheneum, 1971], p. 228).

8. For a recent attempt to refine a rigorous version of utilitarianism, see Peter Singer, *Practical Ethics* (Cambridge: Cambridge University Press, 1979). Rawls is classified at this position because he proposes his theory as a solution to the "priority problem." See John Rawls, *A Theory of Justice* (Cambridge, Mass.: Harvard University Press, 1971), pp. 40–45, 302–03. For some complications and amendments to this claim, see below, sections 4.2, 4.3, and 4.5.

9. See Rawls, *A Theory of Justice*, pp. 34–9. For an influential recent statement see Brian Barry, *Political Argument* (London: Routledge and Kegan

of a plurality of irreconcilably conflicting ultimate principles offers a good recent example of this position.[10]

If we were to reject the first three claims but accept those remaining, we would arrive at position IV, which I have labelled *subjective universalism*. Because this position rejects objective validity, the choice among alternative judgments is admitted to be without justification or support; yet those admittedly subjective values are applied with universalizable consistency, to others as well as to oneself. Although all three objective claims are rejected, universalizability, interpersonal judgment, and judgment of self are accepted. A good example of this position is offered by the early existentialist Sartre in the period exemplified by his essay "Existentialism Is a Humanism." There the arbitrariness of moral choice is clearly asserted as the ultimate meaning of human freedom. Since "man is condemned to be free," his choices are without "any means of justification or excuse."[11] Yet this subjectivity does not undermine universality. In the bare thesis of universalizability, Sartre agrees with Kant: "Although the content of morality is variable, a certain form of this morality is universal." In this sense, one is "to invent the law for himself."[12]

A more extreme variety of subjectivism follows from rejecting claim 4, that of universalizability, in addition to the preceding three. I have reserved the term *relativism* (position V) for this position since its essential character is that it relativizes the application of values to the persons or groups who subscribe to them. Sometimes this position is formulated in terms of conflicting individual positions and sometimes in terms of con-

---

Paul, 1965), chap. 1. For an application to public policy see Arthur Okun, *Equality and Efficiency: The Big Trade-Off* (Washington: The Brookings Institution, 1975).

10. Isaiah Berlin, *Four Essays on Liberty* (Oxford: Oxford University Press, 1969), especially pp. 167–72.

11. Jean-Paul Sartre, "Existentialism Is a Humanism," in Walter Kaufman, ed., *Existentialism: From Dostoevsky to Sartre* (New York: Meridian Books, 1956), p. 295.

12. Ibid., pp. 306–08. As Hare notes in discussing this essay, "Sartre himself is as much a universalist as I am" *(Freedom and Reason*, p. 38).

flicting societal positions or cultures. An example of the former can be found in Edward Westermarck's classic *Ethical Relativity*[13] while the cultural relativists William Graham Sumner and Ruth Benedict exemplify the latter.[14] In both versions the crucial point is that despite the denial of morality in any objective sense, and despite the denial of universalizability, moral judgments are applied interpersonally, but according to the respective values of those judged. For example, while arguing that "nothing but might has ever made right" Sumner relativizes the application of values to the folkways accepted by a given group: "Everything in the mores of a time and place must be regarded as justified with regard to that time and place."[15]

It is worth noting that the dividing line between relativism (position V) and subjective universalism (position IV) will sometimes be difficult to draw. Imagine a moral position whose sole prescription was "judge others by *their* values." Such a position might be construed as a version of subjective universalism (provided that claims 1−3 were rejected), since this formula can be applied universalizably to everyone. Yet its implications would resemble those of relativism (in the familiar interpersonal variant).

Note, however, that the implications of such a variant of subjective universalism do not *precisely* parallel relativism (position V). If X holds universalizably to the normative ethical prescription "judge others by their values," he is thereby committed to prescriptions about how *others* should judge others. It follows from his position that others should also judge others by their (respective) values: not only should X judge Y by Y's values but Y should judge Z by Z's values, etc. No such implication follows from X's commitment to relativism (position V) even

13. Edward Westermarck, *Ethical Relativity* (London: Kegan Paul, Trench and Treubner, 1932; reprinted Westport, Conn.: Greenwood Press, 1970). See, for example, p. 145, where he refers to his view that "the same act can be both good and bad, according as it is approved of by one individual and disapproved of by another."
14. William Graham Sumner, *Folkways* (Boston: Ginnard, 1906), and Ruth Benedict, *Patterns of Culture* (New York: Penguin Books, 1934).
15. Sumner, *Folkways*, p. 58.

though it would follow from this closely parallel variant of position IV, subjective universalism.[16]

Thus far, we have considered rejecting claims 1–4. Now imagine the even more extreme position that would result if we rejected claim 5, interpersonal judgment, as well as all those preceding it. This position has not been the subject of much philosophical speculation. Yet it is, I believe, a theoretical possibility that has a recognizable place in our common moral culture. We will later encounter it among ordinary reasoners.

Alasdair MacIntyre mentions this possibility explicitly, calling it a "private morality" in his critique of the universalizability thesis:

> The fact that a man might on moral grounds refuse to legislate for anyone other than himself (perhaps on the grounds that to do so would be moral arrogance) would by itself be enough to show that not all moral valuation is universalizable. . . . In other words, a man might conduct his moral life without the concept of "duty" and substitute for it the concept of "my duty." But such a private morality would still be a morality.[17]

I will appropriate the term *personalism* (position VI) for such a private morality, for it involves restricting the range of moral judgment to oneself.[18] This position avoids the distinctive issues of non-universalizable interpersonal judgment faced by the relativist. It also avoids the problem faced by the subjective universalist—that of imposing admittedly arbitrary sub-

16. The parallel to relativism is closest if "judge others by their values" is the sole principle in this subjective universalist system. If this subjective universalist has other values in addition that he applies universalizably to everyone regardless of their values, then the contrast with relativism (position V) will be sharper.

17. Alasdair MacIntyre "What Morality Is Not," in G. Wallace and A. D. M. Walker, eds., *The Definition of Morality* (London: Methuen, 1970), p. 30.

18. The term *personalism* has also been employed for a quite different position. See Emanuel Mounier, *Personalism* (London: Routledge and Kegan Paul, 1952).

jective judgments upon others who hold different values. But it avoids these two difficulties at the cost of restricting the application of values that are *sui generis* merely to oneself. While MacIntyre defends the possibility of such a private morality, others might argue that once restricted in this way, such values begin to lose the character of being recognizably moral values at all.

The most extreme position, the *amoralism* of position VII, results from rejection of all six claims. The nihilism discussed by Nietzsche as a transitional phase to the "revaluation of all values" can be thought of as belonging to this position. For the nihilist views life as meaningless, subscribes to no values whatsoever, and has no world view. While some have interpreted Nietzsche himself as a nihilist, we need not enter that controversy here.[19] Whether or not he was a nihilist, the nihilism he made famous offers an example of amoralism.

Another clear description of an amoralist can be found in Theodore Dreiser's account of Frank Cowperwood, the main character in his novel *The Financier*:

> That thing *conscience*, which obsesses and rides some people to destruction, did not trouble him at all. He had no consciousness of what is currently known as sin. There were just two faces to the shield of life from the point of view of his peculiar mind—strength and weakness. Right and wrong? He did not know about those. They were bound up in metaphysical abstrusities about which he did not care to bother. Good and evil? Those were toys of clerics, by which they made money. . . . Morality and immorality? He never considered them. But strength and weakness—oh yes! If you had strength you could protect yourself always and be something. If you were weak—pass quickly to the rear and

19. For the claim that Nietzsche was himself a nihilist, see Arthur C. Danto, *Nietzsche as Philosopher* (New York: Columbia University Press, 1965). For a sharply contrasting interpretation see Richard Schacht, "Nietzsche and Nihilism," in Robert C. Solomon, ed., *Nietzsche: A Collection of Critical Essays* (New York: Anchor, 1973).

get out of the range of the guns. He was strong and he knew it, and somehow he always believed in his star.[20]

Cowperwood, we are told, abjures all moral notions such as conscience, right and wrong, good and evil, morality and immorality. Note, however, that like Nietzsche, he values strength over weakness. Should he be classified as an amoralist or as someone who simply advocates his own morality, which is quite different from the conventional one?

We might, conceivably, attempt to approach this problem by stipulating necessary conditions that a judgment must satisfy if it is to be considered a moral judgment at all. Such an approach would consist in determining the defining conditions of morality as opposed to prudence, taste, etiquette, aesthetics, and other prescriptive or evaluative aspects of human behavior.[21]

The difficulty with such an approach, for our purposes, is that it would rule out, by definitional fiat, some of the very possibilities we intend to investigate. For example, R. M. Hare's proposal that universalizability be incorporated as one of the defining features of moral judgment would rule out, by definition, the relativist and personalist (positions V and VI), who believe they are making moral judgments, but nonuniversalizably. Similarly, consider Hare's proposal that "a man's moral principles" are "those which, in the end, he accepts to guide his life by, even if this involves breaches of subordinate principles such as those of aesthetics or etiquette."[22] This definition would count as moral whatever considerations an apparent amoralist employed to "guide his life by." So long as he could formulate his ultimately guiding considerations, these would become his moral principles and he would thereby, be removed

20. Theodore Dreiser, *The Financier* (New York: New American Library, 1967; original edition, New York: Harper, 1912), p. 240.

21. For some of these contrasts see Neil Cooper, "Morality and Importance," in Wallace and Walker, *The Definition of Morality*, and Philippa Foot, *Virtues and Vices* (Oxford: Basil Blackwell, 1978), especially chap. 13.

22. Hare, *Freedom and Reason*, p. 169.

from the amoralist category (since he would then, by definition, subscribe to some moral principles).

The difficulty, of course, is that the definition of moral as opposed to nonmoral judgment is itself controversial and contested among proponents of the very positions we are attempting to classify. Rather than commit myself to one particular canonical definition, a working strategy for purposes of classification will be to employ the account of the dividing line between moral and nonmoral offered *within* the position to be classified. For example, if Cowperwood believes he has abjured all moral notions, if his admiration for strength does not, in his view, constitute advocacy of an alternative morality, then for our purposes he can be classified as an amoralist. This strategy will permit us to investigate whatever interesting variants present themselves, including advocacy of moral positions that have lost what might appropriately be regarded as some of the defining features of morality—such as universalizability, interpersonal judgment, and other properties. I believe that after an empirical exploration into some of these variants, we will be able to return to these same issues with an enriched sense of the possibilities that emerge when one or another of the putative defining features of morality is denied.

3. An Empirical Exploration

3.1. Moral Dialogues

Dialogues have become fashionable again in moral and political theory. Bruce Ackerman's notion of "constrained conversation" provides the foundation for an impressive liberal theory of social justice.[1] Jürgen Habermas's notion of the "ideal speech situation" provides the foundation for a similarly impressive theory of legitimacy developed within the radical tradition of critical theory.[2] The dialogues about norms or principles envisioned by both of these theorists take place under special idealized conditions—conditions and constraints whose normative appropriateness is not itself the primary subject of the hypothesized dialogues.[3] In that sense they are idealized normative ethical dialogues.

The conversations I will examine here are, by contrast, meta-ethical rather than normative ethical dialogues, and they

---

1. Bruce Ackerman, *Social Justice in the Liberal State* (New Haven and London: Yale University Press, 1970). See especially sections 1–5.
2. Jürgen Habermas, *Legitimation Crisis* (Boston: Beacon Press, 1973), particularly part 3, chap. 3.
3. Note, however, that the conditions of the "ideal speech situation" must be acceptable to its participants. Ackerman's dialogues include no such requirement. For an illuminating discussion of the "ideal speech situation" see Raymond Geuss, *The Idea of a Critical Theory* (Cambridge: Cambridge University Press, 1981), pp. 65–88.

take place with real people under everyday conditions rather than with imaginary people under idealized conditions. Nevertheless, this enterprise and those just mentioned have a common purpose—to probe the coherence and viability of a particular form of *moral and political culture.* I will explore whether certain widespread cultural assumptions that bear on meta-ethical issues produce for our secular Western moral culture— and any liberal state attempting to justify itself from within that culture—a legitimacy crisis according to which that moral culture (and the state operating within it) must de-legitimate itself, that is, must undermine its own legitimacy in the eyes of those who draw the required logical implications from the assumptions that are widely shared.

I believe that the arguments to be explored here will seem familiar. My reason for citing interview materials is not that I believe that the ordinary moral reasoners discussed are strikingly original thinkers. Rather, it is their lack of originality that renders them important for my purposes. They are seriously engaged by the problem of working through familiar implications of familiar assumptions. Because their arguments represent common, sometimes even cliché-ridden philosophical moves, they have a typicality that will permit us to raise issues about the viability and coherence of our shared moral culture.

This study is the outgrowth of an earlier effort to apply Kohlberg's theory to moral and political reasoning.[4] In applying the Kohlberg theory to students and recent graduates at Yale and Cambridge universities, I encountered numerous examples of subjective moral reasoning. As I became increasingly convinced of the difficulty of explaining such responses within the Kohlberg framework, I studied problematical cases in order to develop an alternative theory. This study offers my proposal.

. 4. James Fishkin, Kenneth Keniston, and Catharine MacKinnon, "Moral Reasoning and Political Ideology," *Journal of Personality and Social Psychology* 27 (1973): 109–19. See also James Fishkin, "Relativism, Liberalism and Moral Development," in Richard W. Wilson and Gordon J. Schochet, eds., *Moral Development and Politics* (New York: Praeger, 1980).

I have included interviews here for the light they shed on a theoretical problem: how to classify and evaluate subjective moral reasoning. The interviews reveal a set of arguments that I will explore, not to make empirical claims but to raise certain theoretical issues. First, these arguments are of philosophical interest because they pose a serious challenge to the possibility of an objective or justified morality. Proceeding from common assumptions, our ordinary reasoners map a route to subjectivism that is virtually inescapable. Only through a basic revision in moral culture, through an adjustment in our expectations about what a nonsubjective morality might be like, can we hope to escape their arguments.

Second, these arguments are of theoretical interest to the empirical study of moral reasoning because they reveal how subjectivists have been misclassified. Rather than offering only a phase of inconsistency and confusion, subjectivism may constitute a *resolution* to perplexities and not a source of them. Yet this pattern of resolution, however satisfying, constitutes a challenge to the viability and legitimacy of our shared moral culture.

In this chapter I will attempt to accomplish two goals. First, I will illustrate how the seven logical possibilities presented in chapter 2 can be applied as empirical classifications. Second, I will explore the rationales and arguments that impel some reasoners to subjectivism. I will present their arguments for subjectivism as forcefully as possible and then, in chapter 4, I will show how those arguments may, nevertheless, be overcome—but only through a revision in some of our widely shared moral assumptions.

3.2. The Absolutist

Robert is a thirty-one-year-old Englishman, an unemployed schoolmaster recently converted to Catholicism. He is convinced that there is an a priori solution to all moral questions which is available to all of us. He believes that everyone, regardless of his religion, has a sufficient basis for absolute moral judgment. He says of those who disagree: "Every single one of them that is committing sin now, at one stage, clearly knew by the light of natural conscience, or by the natural light of conscience, that they were committing sin."

He explains that, as he interprets it, "the Catholic principle is that every man has a natural conscience, which gives him a natural light in all these great moral problems which, if he had no other light, is a sufficient light and when he dies and faces his Creator at the particular judgment, he will be judged according to how he has followed this natural conscience." This "natural light" is "sufficient" for "all these great moral problems"; it is universally available and provides unquestionable guidance. It also provides resolutions that have objective validity:

> Q. I'm interested in the nature of this natural light within all of us.
> A. Yes, the natural conscience.
> Q. In other words, it is a guide to a kind of objective truth?
> A. Absolutely, absolutely.
> Q. So then, if all men truly follow this, it should lead them to the same conclusion?
> A. Right.
> Q. . . . if given the same information, or if they're reasoning about the same instance.
> A. If given precisely the same circumstances, if they all followed the light of conscience, they would all arrive at precisely the same conclusion, yes.

Robert accepts objective validity (claim 3), not merely because he uses the word *objective* but because he claims that this "natural light of conscience" provides moral truths accessible in the same way to anyone who consults his conscience. He says, for example, of a particular moral conclusion, "It's going to be as valid as it coincides with what has been objectively worked out."

In addition to accepting the absolutist claim (1) and the objective validity claim (3), Robert accepts all the others as well. He speaks of a "right moral decision" as "the conclusion of a syllogism, the major premise being general principles and the minor being particular circumstances." Such syllogisms are appropriately applied both to his own moral problems and to those of other persons (claims 5 and 6). Because they are based on "general" principles, they are universalizable (claim 4), that is, they are formulated to treat similar cases similarly and should hold for everyone.

He admits, however, that this purely deductive view sometimes leads to difficulties:

> It's difficult to pronounce on moral questions in the abstract, because moral questions are always a mixture of general theoretical principle and particular circumstances in which to apply the principle; and quite obviously the circumstances can considerably influence the principle, but the degree to which the circumstances do influence the principle depends absolutely precisely upon the exact circumstances.

Although the precise circumstances determine which general principle is relevant to a given case, those circumstances never justify exceptions to the chosen principle—provided that the correct principle has been selected. Robert holds, in this way, to the expectation that inviolability (claim 2) can be preserved even though, in particular cases, he encounters difficulty in specifying the principle that would live up to that expectation. In attempting to solve the Heinz dilemma, for example, he searches for an appropriate general classification of Heinz's action that could apply without exception:

> Since his wife's life is at stake, his action is justified. Stealing is in principle, as a general principle, wrong, but just as there is no question that it is right for a man whose family is starving to steal bread to feed his family if he's got absolutely no alternative, so on the same basis it would undoubtedly be right for a man to steal a drug, particularly from a druggist who knows, and who everybody knows, is selling at an exorbitant rate. He would be right to steal the

drug, I mean, stealing is the taking away from a man of—I forget the proper definition of stealing—but it's not an absolutely cut and dried definition, I mean, it's not taking away from a man what is justly his property, even though he has by his genius, or what will you, invented this drug. It would seem to be presented to us, it would seem that Heinz is justified.

Q. What would the major premise be?

A. Oh, the major premise would be—um—what, that stealing is wrong; though, as I said, perhaps the major [premise] is (pause) stealing is wrong when it is a question of taking away from a man what is justly his property.

Q. But, from that, you couldn't deduce the rightness of Heinz's action, could you?

A. Well, um, I think you could, it is not, I mean, I—there are absolutely clear principles on this, I mean, I don't know them but there are—if you go to certain (pause) textbooks of moral principles in which you could look up the objective principles to apply in a case like this. The classic exception to the broad rule that stealing is wrong is the man feeding his starving family when there's no other way. That's not wrong, and it would seem to me that comes basically into the same category.

Even though Robert cannot specify the appropriate general principle for resolving this dilemma, he has no doubts of its existence. In the appropriate "textbooks" we should be able to find the principle that holds without exception (unlike the too "broad" rule that "stealing is wrong") and that covers this "category" of action: "Man's sense of what is justice has undoubtedly been worked out on the subject—it's not as though we're completely, you know, in the fog if we made up our minds to go and look up the question."

3.3. The Rigorist

Patrick is a Cambridge undergraduate. His moral principles are inviolable: it is always wrong, he believes, to violate or override a principle, even when it conflicts with other principles. Patrick is sophisticated enough to know that principles may conflict with one another in particular situations, but he concludes from this fact that in such cases every alternative must be wrong. Cases of that kind, he believes, define tragedy.

He mentions the ancient example of Agamemnon. On the one hand, he says, "as the leader of the fleet," Agamemnon "had a duty to make sure it [the war effort] was successful." But Agamemnon found himself, on the other hand, in a situation where "the only way of doing this was sacrificing his daughter." Of course, "as a father . . . and indeed as a person in general, he mustn't go around killing other persons." Here is Agamemnon's tragic choice: "There are two quite clear obligations upon him and it's that not both can be fulfilled."

In such situations, Patrick believes, *none* of the alternatives would be right, for each would involve violation of an inviolable obligation. "There are some cases," he explains, "in which one is in a situation in which none of the possible courses of action are right, and then that's just bad luck, or bad judgment or something."

In such unfortunate cases, if you live up to one claim, the obligation to live up to the incompatible claim does not "vanish." "The obligation you have to follow one course of action," he explains, "is not canceled out by your stronger obligation to carry out a different and incompatible course of action." This is why he believes that in such situations "none of the possible courses of action are right."

Patrick's view that it would be wrong to violate any of these obligations—even when they conflict with one another— explains his somewhat cryptic reaction to the question of whether "Heinz did the right thing." "If there was a right thing," Patrick responds, "he certainly did it. It's more that, in that situation, nothing one could do would be right."

He admits that when one is in such a situation—a situation reminiscent of the tragedy of Agamemnon—one can attempt to act on the better option. "You can try," he says, "and take the best combination." One course may indeed be more compelling than the other. "Sometimes it will be that one just knows that one must do one of them."

His point, however, is that the other obligation does not "vanish without trace—it remains there." As a result, "one has, for example, a duty to be sorry about it, to make reparations for it, and so on as if one had done it for no very good reason."

A person should thus treat the violation of one of the conflicting principles (Heinz's violation, for example, of the prohibition against stealing) as a "wrong" committed "just as if one had done it for no very good reason." It is in this sense that in situations where violating one principle or another is unavoidable, "nothing one could do would be right." Objective principles are thus inviolable, according to Patrick, because it is always wrong to violate them.

In addition to affirming the inviolable character of his principles, he asserts that they can be supported with "reasons" but in a way that is always open to controversy and possible disagreement. For example, in his response to the Heinz dilemma, he arrives at the following point:

A. Well, one just has the idea that saving someone's life matters more than someone else's making money.

Q. How would you justify that idea: what are the grounds of that idea?

A. Maybe it is itself a ground and has no need of other grounds. There might be plausible counterexamples clearly, but . . . Someone who *really* needs the grounds for that, will, such a person, I would feel wouldn't accept anything I would say, so I just wouldn't say anything. I don't know, maybe that's where it rests, and maybe one could say something more.

Although he does not expect his moral arguments to be universally convincing, he does believe there is a weaker sense in which they are "objective":

> It's objective like this: that when one's arguing a moral case with someone, one learns the sort of considerations that are relevant, even if one can't always find them. And you give reasons, and they're good reasons and in the end you come to some agreement.

He contrasts this sense of objectivity with that involved in matters of fact such as questions of numbers:

> It's not that if it's lack of objectivity in [matters of] size, all one can do is take one's stand and stay there. There are reasons, but if you're asking is there a right answer always, the answer's no.

Although Patrick holds to his principles inviolably, he thus recognizes that they are controversial and that reasonable persons may disagree about them. Because they apply inviolably, it is obvious that Patrick's position includes the claims of universalizability, interpersonal judgment, and judgment of self. Hence, while rejecting the absolutist claim to rationally unquestionable principles, his position conforms to all five of the remaining claims required for position II, rigorism.

3.4. The Minimal Objectivist

Ron is a Yale graduate student. Like Patrick, he emphasizes the possibilities for reasonable disagreement in ethical matters. After prescribing that Heinz "should have done it" (stolen the drug to save his wife's life), he raises this issue:

> But if somebody disagreed with him and said that Heinz's argument was wrong because his value premises were wrong, could such an argument be refuted by Heinz? Or by me? Probably not, because there would be no way of demonstratably establishing the premises. Therefore it's, you know, in that sense, not ultimate, not absolute.

He explains that by this he means

> that it can't be, well, *proven*. Because it ought to be possible to make a coherent argument for another position—an ar-

gument that I probably wouldn't agree with because I'd disagree with the premises. But my disagreeing with it and it's being an incoherent argument are two different things.

Even though he cannot "prove" his principles, he explains:

And yet, see I'm willing to affirm my value premises as being value premises—as being things that I believe in as standards of making moral judgments.

Such standards, he explains, are valid in the sense that he believes them to have truth value:

I mean to assert a universal truth. But at the same time, you know, I recognize that that assertion is an assertion, is something I believe. . . . If another person makes a different assertion, then it's certainly possible to argue about, it's certainly possible to discuss it with him, but there's no way I can prove he's wrong.

If he were to argue with a Nazi, for example, they would probably "agree on the conclusion that our values are, in fact, opposed," he says. "To the Nazi I'm a bad person."

"But see," he emphasizes, "that's different from saying that his values are just as good as mine. That kind of viewpoint, if you take that kind of viewpoint, then moral discourse becomes impossible. But also, if you take the viewpoint that moral values are absolute in the sense of being demonstrable, moral discourse isn't really possible."

"Moral discourse is only possible," he concludes, "insofar as there's something to discuss." There would not be "something to discuss" if he accepted that anyone else's reasons—including the Nazi's—were as good as his own. Neither would there be anything to discuss if values were ultimately "demonstrable"; then, some positions would be proved wrong and others proved right, and all such moral questions would be conclusively settled.

What Ron seems to be asserting is a middle ground between the position that anyone's values are as good as anyone else's and the position that "absolutes" can be "proved." In this middle ground there is room for disagreement—but also for reasoned persuasion.

"If somebody wants to know why he should believe what I believe," he says, "then I give him the sort of arguments that back up my beliefs and hope to convince him." Ron will "make a case for them," he says, "on the basis of the substance of the beliefs."

The resulting process is not conclusive but also not entirely irrational. "Maybe," Ron says, "he adopts my beliefs because then he has my reasons for believing them—or why anyone should believe them." In this sense Ron's values are "beliefs"; he thinks he can argue for them even though he cannot "prove" them. His values are not the private "tastes" we will find among our subjective cases. Rather, they are supported by reasons and arguments that he is recommending to everyone.

Yet Ron also differs in one important way from the rigorist discussed in the last section. He regards his values as "working principles" that hold "ceteris paribus" for cases of conflict:

> You make the affirmation [of a moral principle] as an affirmation for which you're responsible and you get to, in principle, you get to get what you want. There may be reasons why you can't get what you want—like it may not be possible in the present situation, or it may harm other people. But when you can't get what you want, there's always a reason for it. There's sort of a ceteris paribus state of affairs that you can't, but perhaps you should—that's my value, I mean, that involves value premises on my part.

Hence principles are subject to exceptions or overridings for "reasons" such as "it may harm other people"; they hold "ceteris paribus" for exceptions that involve "value premises on my part." Ron's principles are "valid" as "universal truths" yet they are not inviolable. He cannot "prove" them, yet he is willing to "affirm" them for "reasons." Although he asserts their validity, he subscribes to neither of the two stronger objectivist claims (inviolability and absolutism). Hence he offers an example of the minimal objectivist position.

3.5. The Subjective Universalist

Brian, a Yale undergraduate, begins his response to the Heinz dilemma by questioning whether he can offer a moral response to it: "I've got a whole problem. I'm not quite sure what moral criteria are. I would do it [steal the drug if in Heinz's position]. I'm not sure what it means to say that it's right." He explains:

> To me morality has a connotation of some kind of absoluteness. Because it seems to me that's the only thing which distinguishes it from any other value. For instance . . . I say I don't like asparagus and you don't pursue me on that value. I say I don't like this and you say, well, why not proclaim it moral or immoral. I don't see the distinction.

He does not see the distinction between judgments of taste, such as liking asparagus, and moral judgments. The interview continues:

> Q. The distinction between what?
> A. Between asparagus and man: between why I should, say, not have to be pursued on the subject that I dislike asparagus but that, somehow, I can be pursued on the subject of why I dislike what you call a moral question. They both come to me from the same place—which is somewhere in the middle of my stomach. You know somehow this is what I feel. And I don't see that I can justify. Not only can't I see that I can justify it, I don't feel any necessity to justify it—in any other terms.

Because he cannot see the distinction, he assimilates both moral judgments and those of taste (such as his dislike of asparagus) to the same model of unrationalized, purely emotive preference: "They both come to me from the same place—which is somewhere in the middle of my stomach."

Despite his assimilation of moral judgments to those of taste, Brian feels a need to try to be "consistent" about moral judgments. He even identifies consistency (discussed as treating relevantly similar cases similarly) as a defining feature (the "mark") of moral reasoning. If he is to find some basis for his ultimate assumptions, a "stopping point" for the chain of questions he can raise about his values, then he concludes:

> Everything else is liable to reason after that point, assuming you find consistency the mark of moral reasoning. Because that's what logic is most involved with, the logic I know.

While he does subscribe to consistency, it is always possible, he feels, to differentiate situations:

> To be reasonable or logical I have to be consistent. You see, [to] the question of consistency I would say, "Yes, my feeling is, I should be consistent." But I can get out of acting consistently by saying every situation is different.

He explains:

> To make two situations similar, you have to abstract something from them. Whatever you leave behind is the difference between them. If nothing else, the time between them. I've grown older or something. So it's impossible to act consistently even if I wanted to, since every situation is different.

But then this conclusion appears too strong:

> The problem is, can you really abstract the significant principles and leave off the unimportant ones? If you could, then, yeah, I probably act consistently.

While the possibilities for further differentiation sometimes appear to make consistency impossible (or trivial as a requirement), Brian is insistent that he judges himself by the same criteria he applies to others:

But I don't think I judge myself any differently than I judge—in different *terms* than I judge—anyone else. Obviously, I judge differently, but I don't think on different terms.

In spite of his difficulties in determining relevant similarity, he applies to himself the same values, the same "terms" for judging, that he applies to others. In this sense he subscribes to universalizability, judgment of others, and judgment of self. Because he views consistency as the "mark of moral reasoning" and because he feels he "should be consistent," I will classify him as a universalist, despite his recognition that apparently similar acts can always be further differentiated.

3.6. The Relativist

Sam is a nineteen-year-old Yale undergraduate. His basic position, worked out after long reflection, is:

> Really, there is no ultimate justification or ultimate value in any one system of ethics. The value that some people place on good and the value that other people place on good can be in contradiction to one another, and there is no ultimate or absolute arbiter between the two.

He has changed, he says, from viewing his values as "absolute" external creations to viewing them as subjective "internal" creations—creations that are justified "simply by the fact that I have them."

"The only justification that I would seek to give my values now," he explains, "is that they're personal values or tastes or preferences of mine for ways of acting." He adds, "I don't have to justify them and they don't have to be consistent."

"In terms of defending them to someone else," he concludes, "the only defense I have to give is that I acted in such and such a way because I *wanted* to act in such a way—with little or no other justification for having acted that way."

With this realization, he views his "taste" for honesty, for example, as having no more justification than his "taste" for T-bone steaks: "I prefer a T-bone steak to a sirloin because we used to have T-bones instead of sirloins. In the same sense, I grew up and developed a taste for honesty. That's as far as I can take it."

He should not have to "say that I'm honest because it's the rational or godly or moral thing to do." He gets "into trouble," he says, with claims of that kind. "The 'I' in that statement ["I'm honest because"] should be enough to support it without having to add a 'because' at the end."

But his own assertion of value (without a "because" at the end) is only "enough" to "support it" for himself. Without "an ultimate or absolute arbiter" to legislate between conflicting views, he tries to give the values of others the same standing. "I equate any one belief with any other belief, or any set of values with any other set of values."

About values, in general, he says, "Their basis is all arbitrary and maybe one is a little bit more internally consistent or logical than the others. Or maybe one is a little bit more appealing than the others to one person rather than another. But in an intellectual sense, to me, they're all as valid as the other."

"Heinz," for example, "did what he did as a means to an end which he placed above other ends. So he said that his action was necessary or was right—was the lesser of two evils. On the other hand, the druggist is not really concerned about the coming death of Mrs. Heinz and places some type of value upon personal property."

Can he condemn the druggist for his refusal to save the life of Mrs. Heinz? "I think it would be very unfair," he concludes, "to impose upon the druggist the valuation or the idea that he has to value Mrs. Heinz's life over his own satisfaction—over his own personal enrichment."

To "impose" the value of Mrs. Heinz's life on the druggist would be to ignore the druggist's own morality—a morality that (Sam assumes) places a "value upon personal property." To judge the druggist according to values different from the ones that he (the druggist) believes in would, Sam suggests, be "unfair".

Sam's position becomes clearest when he deals with the Plague problem (dilemma 4, appendix D): the decision of a medieval city to contain the ravages of the Plague by walling up those in the affected houses (condemning those inside to death but saving more lives than would have survived otherwise):

> To the people who are doing the walling up—the authorities of the city—and to, I suppose, the people who survived, the action was probably seen as good in that it prevented the plague from spreading. To the people who were walled up but who didn't have the plague, the action was probably seen as bad, and not, you know, not something that should have been done, something which was evil, or morally reprehensible.

Sam attempts to affirm all these conflicting evaluations simultaneously:

> I'm looking at it from the standpoint that values of actions are given by people in certain situations, not that the values placed upon actions are given by any sort of absolute arbiter, or absolute yardstick. So that in that case the action was both good and evil, good and bad, you know, depending on whose viewpoint you're looking from.

He affirms these conflicting judgments from an "overview, from somewhere outside" the situation. He explains:

> So that I really don't think there's a "legitimate" thing to do in that situation, that I can only look at that situation from an overview, from somewhere outside of it, and that there isn't a right thing to do and a wrong thing to do. There's only a thing for one set of people to do to try and preserve themselves, and a thing for another set of people to do to try and preserve themselves.

In concluding from this "overview" that "the action was both good and evil, good and bad, you know, depending on whose viewpoint you're looking from," Sam embraces the position that I call relativism (position V). In addition to denying the other preceding claims (absolutism, inviolability, objective validity), he denies universalizability. He does not apply any one set of values with universalizable consistency to everyone but tries to affirm all the conflicting values applied to the situation by the various actors in it. It is in that sense that an action can be *"both* good and evil," etc. (from these various conflicting perspectives). Since Sam clearly embraces interpersonal judgment and judgment of self, the last two claims, he conforms to position V, relativism.

3.7. The Personalist

Stephen is a Cambridge undergraduate studying medicine. He finds himself grappling with the paradox of attempting to say that (in some sense) it is "bad" to make judgments of "good" and "bad":

> I think that the mistake my parents made, and I mean I don't want to keep qualifying these words, but if I use the word "mistake" I am not saying, I'm not pretending that I'm right, I'm just talking about myself now although I'm quite aware that I may change. So, you know, let's get that one straight, okay? Now I think the mistake many parents make is to make judgments of good and bad, and I think that the ills of the world could probably be tied down to making judgments of good and bad. I mean it's really as simple as that, and I don't, I try not to make such judgments myself, and I would prefer to live in a world where people didn't make those judgements. And where I didn't make those judgments.

Although he is not willing to force others to accommodate to his own views, Stephen feels compelled to accommodate his own views to those of others—as a way of "respecting" the opinions of others. He explains that to "rip off" or steal would involve imposing his views of right and wrong on others, namely, those stolen from (provided they believe they have the right to the object as well). Their view of ownership "cancels" any "right" which he thinks he might have to the same object:

> *Q.* But in this society, what's wrong with "ripping off" from another person?
>
> *A.* Well, that involves me in saying that I have a right to the thing that he hasn't. I mean and I don't think there's any demonstration, I mean whatever I believe is a right I have, I should respect his opinion too, even if I disagree with it. And if he thinks he should own that piece of property, then I think he should own that piece of property. Then I don't think, I mean I think that cancels my right to the object, because I would be doing him harm if I took the object.

Similarly, he cannot impose on others a political ideology such as "communism" (which he might otherwise feel sympathy toward), because he has no right to "dictate to some capitalist that communism was the right system for him." He is left only with deciding for himself, and if imposed upon, he must "turn the other cheek":

> Even if I believed in, say, communism, as a political system, the way I am now, I wouldn't believe that that would give me a right to dictate to some capitalist that communism was the right system for him. And see, I think what a lot of people don't get to is the point of saying, "Well, okay, the capitalist system treads on me, but I won't tread on it . . ." I think one has to, one has to really sort of, I think Christ was onto this, too, you know, one really does have to turn the other cheek, if you think you've been hurt.

Stephen's effort to avoid "dictating" to others is part of his general position that he is only "capable of making judgments about judgments for myself." In other words, because he regards himself as having an insufficient basis for judging others, he doesn't believe that he should judge them at all—even in terms of their own preferences or perspectives.

I only think that I am capable of making judgments for myself, and I'm, I mean, equally only capable of making judgments about judgments for myself. I mean I wouldn't like to apply it to any other, anybody else's life. I mean, I don't know if it's right, if I was to say that was right then I would already be making as far as I was concerned judgments about every action that there is, which is something that I set out to avoid doing in the beginning.

His response to the Heinz dilemma reveals further how his restriction of the sphere of moral judgment to himself is linked to the fallibility and mutability that he attributes to his own judgment:

A. Well, I could only say what I would do in a similar situation. I mean I don't think that I can judge what other people do as right or wrong. I can say whether I thought it was right or wrong for myself.

Q. Could you just explain just a bit why it is you feel you can't judge what other, what's right or wrong for somebody else?

A. Because I make, because I've made too many mistakes of my own to be able to think that I've arrived at a point where I'm safe enough to judge other people. For one thing I'm developing very fast in my head and so I don't really know what I'm going to think in a year's time. So I wouldn't like to make any absolute judgments. I mean I could only say what I think of it at this moment, for myself in a similar situation.

He explains that because he is continually changing, "I'm prepared only to be wrong for myself." While he might hope that others follow his advice, it does not have any "justification"; he is not "sure" enough to "be in a state to judge for anybody else." He continues his response to the Heinz dilemma as follows:

A. Well, if you ask me to judge the action, Heinz's action, I can judge what I would do in the situation, and if Heinz came to me for advice, I would explain to him what I would do and why I would do it. But I wouldn't, I mean, I could make a judgment if you ask me what my answer is, I think Heinz was right. But it's not a judgment I think there's any justification for. So you can have it as my answer, but I wouldn't think that my answer is applicable to anybody else's life. Or actions.

Q. So it's not applicable at all, or they wouldn't be bound or shouldn't, you wouldn't say that they should be bound by those considerations?

A. No, I wouldn't say they shouldn't, I hope they would. But I'm not sure about that. I mean it would please me very much if everybody could get there, including myself. I think we'd have a marvelous time. Everybody. But I'm not sure that I'm right even for myself, as I said, because I develop, and maybe in five years' time I won't think the same thing. So I'm prepared only to be wrong for myself. Certainly I wouldn't be in a state to judge for anybody else.

Because Stephen does not view his admittedly subjective moral judgments as "applicable" to anybody else, he exemplifies position VI, personalism. His position can be defined, first, by the denial of claims 1–5, including most notably the claim of interpersonal judgment, and second, by the acceptance of the one remaining claim, judgment of self.

3.8. The Amoralist

Harvey is an American mathematician doing graduate work at Cambridge. In responding to the Heinz dilemma, he appears at first to use the moral language of "should" and "ought." It soon becomes apparent, however, that he uses these words only in a purely instrumental sense for the satisfaction of wants or preferences. He responds to the dilemma about whether Heinz should steal the drug in order to save his wife's life:

A. Well, if I can't get it and I ask him, and he won't give it to me, and there's no other way to get it, I'd steal it, or

Heinz should steal it, unless he wants his wife to die, then he shouldn't steal it.

Q. Why is that?

A. Well, if he wants, if the drug is needed for the wife, right, if he wants the wife to live, then he should steal the drug so he can give it to the wife so she can live. If he wants her to die, then he shouldn't do that. Or he shouldn't have to, he wouldn't—I wouldn't, if I wanted her to die.

Q. Would it be *right* to let her die if you could save her life?

A. Well, if I wanted to let her die, well, yes, of course.

Q. If you wanted to let her die, it would be right to let her die?

A. Well, no. I never say it's right or wrong. I say, "I want to let her die so I let her die." In other words, if there was something that I could do to save her, I wouldn't do it.

When asked further whether any of these actions might be "right or wrong," he responds: "Well, no. It depends if I feel that I wanted something that might be good. There's no question of right or wrong." His use of the word "good" here, I assume, is merely in the sense of desirable, or tending to satisfy preferences, not in any moral sense. He sees no question in this dilemma other than that of the satisfaction of one's own wants.

Harvey attempts to differentiate these egoistic judgments, which he is willing to make, from the "moral" judgments that he is not willing to make. He does not see himself as advocating a morality but as attempting to do without one. "There is no question of right or wrong," he explains. "I mean, you can say there's right or wrong for me or right or wrong for you. But I'm just saying there's not really any question of right or wrong—a sense of values prior to the situation where you say according to this: 'this is wrong' or 'this is right.'"

Harvey rejects "a sense of values prior to the situation" because he cannot find a basis for "deriving" reasons. In looking for such a basis, he "can't get back to something fundamental. It's all very amorphous."

As a result, Harvey is sure that in "ethics" (as in "sociology" and "philosophy"), "you'll always have different schools fighting." "At least in science," he explains, "one presumes that you have general criteria of reproducibility—of being able to present the experiment and do it over and over again and have the same result—a sort of constancy with the universe."

"In subjects like sociology and ethics," on the other hand, "it's more a matter of personal taste and we don't really have good analytical criteria. We don't have anything that's unarguable. You'll always have different schools fighting. That's what the history of the subject will be."

Believing that it's "a matter of personal taste," Harvey tries to suppress entirely the process of giving reasons—even for his personal likes and dislikes. He never decides general questions but attempts to confront particular situations in their concrete immediacy. "You can't really decide beforehand," he believes, because you cannot know "what you're going to want to do until you decide it at that moment." His goal is a kind of unreasoned spontaneity. "Right away," he says, "I like something or not. Or I try to be like that. There's never really a reason—you can always contradict reasons."

In attempting to do without reasons, he is left only with judgments of immediate want-satisfaction of the kind he offered to Heinz: "If he wants the wife to live then he should steal the drug. . . . If he wants her to die, then he shouldn't do that. . . . I never say it's right or wrong."

In the last several sections I have introduced each position in the scheme with a detailed illustration. Further issues in the empirical application of these classifications are explored in appendix B. Now we are in a position to probe the arguments underlying adoption of the subjectivist positions.

3.9. The First Argument: The Quest for Foundations

"The thing that bothers me," says Brian (our subjective universalist), "is that word 'justification.' Because, to me, justification means that there is something *back there* that we have all agreed on . . . and then you show me logically how those justifying elements agree with your actions."

"And I simply don't understand what is back there," he continues, "how anything has that power of justification other than the revelation of God—which you can't deny, by definition. Otherwise, I don't see how any phrase you happen to drop carries with it the power of justification."

He tries to spell out the difficulty more precisely: "I assume when you say 'justify' you're talking about 'justify' using logic and using reason and using certain definitions. My problem is reason can't deal with that."

The attempt to use reason is overwhelmed, he believes, by a kind of "infinite regress." "If you say, 'Justify Z in terms of Y,' and I say, 'Well, explain Y or defend Y,' and you end up using X, and so forth and so on, at no point can you *stop*. At the point where you "stop," Brian explains: "You have to say 'just because.' And once you get to that point, that's not open to reason."

At that point the rationales are merely, " 'because I think that's right' or 'I feel that's right.' " Brian agrees that "you need something more than that to stop." His problem is that "reason does not allow anything. I don't think there is anything. . . . I don't even think anyone's been able to define for me God, or the stopping point, or whatever—the procedure to find the stopping point."

While "everything else is liable to reason *after* that point— assuming you find consistency the mark of moral reasoning," his problem is that he sees no basis for his most fundamental assumptions.

But what kind of basis is he searching for? Brian mentions that many cultures probably share some fundamental values such as "that there are certain conditions in which you do not kill somebody else" (although "that in no way says that they all agree on any given set of conditions"). But even if there were agreement on the conditions for not killing, Brian says, "in order to make it meaningful to me, you would have to show that

that was somehow *inherent* in the structure of the animal—the human animal almost *had* to agree not to kill under these circumstances for whatever reasons."

Brian is seeking a kind of undeniable necessity for his basic moral assumptions—something with the "power of justification" or the irrefutable character of "moral revelation." In fact, as he considers the question, he concludes that even if conditions for not killing were "somehow inherent in the structure of the animal," he would *still* not have found a sufficient basis. For even if men somehow found it necessary to agree, he would conclude, "That's no moral basis, that's not moral revelation. That's a genetic determination."

Without an irrefutable basis in, for example, "moral revelation," he feels driven to the conclusion that his ultimate premises can be no better—and no worse—than anyone else's. "How can one say, 'I don't have the revealed word of God, I don't know what is truth, I realize that my resources are exactly symmetrical with the other guy who I'm condemning, but somehow he's wrong and I'm right'? I would like to see some argument for that, some consistent argument for that. And I don't see how one can even devise such an argument, just because of the nature of reason."

Brian thus reaches the conclusion, discussed earlier, that others' values are as valid as his own: "My view would be the other guy has a perfectly, as sound a ground as I do for acting, and I can't make any value judgment of him other than the fact that I don't like what he's doing."

Stephen, our personalist, is led to a subjective position by a similar search for assumptions that cannot rationally be denied. It is his unsuccessful quest for such an "ultimate framework" that leads him to conclude "that I wouldn't be in a state to judge for anybody else."

As in Brian's case, the arbitrariness of his basic assumptions is revealed by a seemingly infinite regress of questions. In describing his Catholic upbringing he says, "God was a belief and if you believed in it, that was cool. And you followed those rules, if that's what you believed He wanted you to do. And if you didn't believe in God, well, you had to go away and find something else."

Stephen's skepticism arises from the fact that "whenever you got to an impasse—which is the sort of thing you get to when you analyze everything—you suddenly came to a great big abyss, and you know there's nothing that's going to fill it to enable you to get to the other side. If there is another side. And whenever that came, it would always end up being filled in by your belief in God." He finds this way of resolving questions unconvincing: "Doesn't it sound unreasonable whenever you're stuck, to go and appeal to God? And it does, it really does."

"But everything else," Stephen says, "proved to be the same, to the touch, if you like. I would take something up as possibly leading to a sort of ultimate framework, and would come to exactly the same emotional disillusionments with it." Each assumption, in turn, appears open to question: "Like I'd like to climb up a ladder and at a certain point you'd say, 'Am I ever going to get to the end?' And the answer was always, 'Doesn't look like it.'"

The "end" of the questioning seems unreachable to Stephen because he could never "come to the point that you got to the question that was self-answering or something like that—some point where there would obviously be a terminus." "And it never looked like coming," Stephen says of this deductive stopping point. "Whenever there was a question, you'd provide an answer, and then, more or less by definition, you'd have to explain the answer and then you'd have to explain the explanation. And so on. So I ended up not believing in anything."

Harvey, our amoralist, also connects his subjective position to the lack of irrefutable basic assumptions. He is attracted to logic because "things are either true or false. It's decidable. You can decide whether a proof is correct or incorrect." The situation is quite different in ethics and philosophy: "It's endless arguments because you can never say for sure that yours is a better argument than somebody else's. It's a matter of personal choice, isn't it?"

As a result, controversies are never settled: "In subjects like sociology and ethics . . . and philosophy it's more a matter of personal taste and we don't really have good analytical criteria—*we don't have anything that's unarguable* [emphasis added]. You'll always have different schools fighting. That's what the history of the subject will be."

Any criteria that may seem "absolute" are really based, at bottom, on choices that are no more than "personal taste." "Trying to present foundations for morals and ethics on a broad enough level—unless it's tautology and unless it depends on formal rules of deduction . . . it won't go to the a priori axioms or the a priori statements. I don't think you can get any for morals— any a priori foundation before any fact. It's all empty from that point of view. You can only have implicational or tautological statements about such things—just like in any system."

Because there is no "a priori foundation," Harvey concludes that one cannot give "reasons" in ethics at all. Harvey explains that "by 'reason' I mean some kind of rationale derived from some kind of principle." In this sense he believes, "You really can't give reasons. It's an infinite regress: you say 'I did this because of this.' And why is that? 'Because of this.' You can never get back to something *fundamental*—for me, I mean, I can't get back to something fundamental. It's all very amorphous."

Sam, our relativist, also reaches his position through a questioning of "ultimate" assumptions. He has recently come to the realization "that, really, there is no ultimate justification or ultimate value in any one system of ethics and that the value that some people place on good and the value that other people place on good can be in contradiction to one another and there is no ultimate or absolute arbiter between the two."

Without such an "absolute arbiter" he feels disarmed from "imposing" his values on others at all. No longer can he "say that my values are better than a set of values that someone else may hold because my values are rational and because my values come from a religious context which is ultimately based on God, because God is absolute truth, and so on."

No longer can he make such arguments. But without such ultimate support his values are no longer moral values in the same sense; they are asserted merely as personal "tastes." "I still hold those values that I held, but I would really hesitate now to call them moral values." They are no longer values that have any justification: "The only justification that I would seek to give my values now is that they're personal values or tastes or preferences of mine for ways of acting, and I don't have to justify them and they don't have to be consistent."

He does not claim any justification for his values because he lacks an "ultimate basis" for them. His "taste for honesty" has no more basis than his "taste for T-bone steaks": "I grew up and developed a taste for honesty—that's as far as I can take it. . . . As soon as I attempt to take it any farther and say that I'm honest because it's the rational or godly or moral thing to do, I get into trouble."

"Once you fall into the trap," he explains, "of having to seek support from outside, once you fall into the trap of basing something on an absolute outside of yourself or outside of the world or whatever—such as God or Truth or Reason—then as soon as that absolute is brought into question, then your system of values crumbles."

He attempts to avoid this crumbling of his values by not positing, in the first place, any "external" support for them. "I'm attempting to justify my values simply by the fact that I have them." Instead of attempting to complete the statement, "I'm honest because . . . ," he now takes the view that "the 'I' in that statement should be enough to support it without having to add a 'because' at the end." These values without a "because" are mere personal tastes; without an absolute justification, he views them as having no justification. His system of values can no longer "crumble"—only because he claims no support for them.

Jonathan, a Yale undergraduate planning to attend business school after graduation, mentions a similar chain of questioning: "In any argument you can say, 'Why?' 'Why?' 'Why?' and then there's a point where [the only answer is] 'Because.'"

He cannot see any convincing end to this recurring demand for justification, so he ends by believing only in "self-interest," which he regards as a departure from morality (and not a version of it):

> I don't think there is any religious basis because I don't believe in any religions that I've ever heard. And I suppose I haven't heard any nonreligious, nonspiritual purely logical explanation for why such a right and wrong should exist. It comes down to: if it's truly against a man's self-interest to act in a "moral" way, who the hell gives a damn about morality? How could you possibly expect a man to act against his self-interest when himself is all he has—to be moral?

These cases all offer variants of one basic argument: because moral judgments are not, in some sense, rationally unquestionable, they must be subjective. Brian, for example, is looking for assumptions that have "the power of justification"—assumptions that "you can't deny, by definition." Without such assumptions, he views his values as having no justification whatsoever.

Stephen is also searching for an undeniable "ultimate framework": "the question that was self-answering or something like that." For Harvey, without something "fundamental" or "unarguable" there is no room for "reason" in ethics at all. Similarly, "without an absolute arbiter" Sam regards all his values as "personal tastes," having no more justification than his tastes for foods.

Each of these reasoners argues from an assumption about one of the necessary conditions that a moral position must satisfy if it is to be objectively valid—if, in other words, it is to avoid subjectivism in the sense defined by any of our last four positions. These reasoners then argue from the lack of that necessary condition to the subjective or arbitrary character of their moral positions. In the case of the first argument, this expectation can be identified as:

> *Expectation 1*: An objectively valid moral position must have a basis that is rationally unquestionable.

In the sections that follow I will introduce other expectations about an objectively valid (nonsubjective) position that perform a parallel role in the other arguments for subjectivism. Once we have identified each of these expectations, we will be in a position to discuss the more general implications of this recurring pattern of argument.

3.10. The Second Argument: Confronting Moral Complexity

"I do not believe that there is or can be any small, or even very large, set of fundamental principles from which you can deduce moral theorems or moral laws which people or society 'should' guide themselves by," asserts Doug, a recent Yale student planning to do graduate work in computer science. Doug draws on his extensive scientific background in explaining his philosophy. "Society is extremely complicated," he begins. "The behavior of an individual human cell is extraordinarily complex. The behavior of the aggregate of billions of cells, which is one human being, is vastly more complex. And the behavior of humanity as a whole, which is a collection of billions of vastly complexly behaving human beings, is astronomically still more complex."

Given this complexity, "The first meaning of my statement that there are no such sets of principles is this: that no reasonably small set of principles could possibly capture unambiguously and to everyone's agreement in every situation the astronomically complex, and for the most part astronomically ambiguous, situations that people are required to make decisions on every day."

With some hyperbole he continues, "There is no small set of principles, in no set of volumes, in no five books of principles, in no five libraries of principles, in no five libraries of single sentence, or single paragraph sets of independent principles, viewed as rigid laws, could there be enough information to adequately describe or take account of the tremendous complexity."

The difficulty of designing moral principles that could adequately apply as "rigid laws" is such that "even if you believed that some God could set down a set of principles which would unambiguously and completely determine the proper moral decision in any situation . . . such a set of principles would not be small and no human or set of humans could possibly hold it all in his mind at once. And if he could, he couldn't possibly spend the time to make such a decision. It would take him a trillion years to evaluate the moral principles properly."

But without such an adequate set of "rigid laws" Doug is left only with "rules of thumb," which he chooses "for convenience only" and which, he believes, reflect nothing more than "the arbitrariness of the construction of my own psychology." Because principles, if applied *"rigidly,"* must be inadequate to the "complexity" of the human situation, he believes that there are no "fundamental principles . . . moral theorems or moral laws which people or society 'should' guide themselves by."

Jonathan also argues for subjectivism by asserting that there are no "absolute" values that are "inviolable." For the main philosophical alternative that he sees to subjectivism is this possibility: "I would imagine that in many religions there are absolute values which are more important than self-interest—which are inviolable." He offers the Ten Commandments as an example.

But he does not believe in such "absolute values" because "there are times when any two values can conflict." He explains, "When you have to make a decision between conflicting principles and you decide that one principle always survives the conflict, then that principle is the inviolable one and that's the one which you have to build your system on."

For example, "Certainly it's not logical [by which he apparently means something like "reasonable"] to believe that you can never steal under any circumstances . . . if human life were at stake . . . then you'd say, well, you can never steal unless you save a human life. And then if you're talking about human life, I think there are some times when you could, perhaps, kill a person justly—maybe in saving other human lives."

He continues to envision possible exceptions: "So the value 'Never kill anyone at all' wouldn't be good, and perhaps 'Maximize the total number of lives' might be the one which you might want to abide by—which would have no exceptions."

But this last position must also be overridden, he believes, because "the number of lives, in itself, is not necessarily the most important point. It's the value of those individual human lives." For example, he speculates that "two great men" might be more important than "six rotten men."

However, he offers these values only as examples. For he believes the only principle that might be "inviolable" is "self-interest," and he does not regard that as a moral principle at all. In explaining that the "inviolable" principle is "the one which you have to build your system on," he adds:

> And so if I had a moral system I would build it upon self-interest, but it seems that to build a moral system totally upon self-interest is redundant—because then when you'd say people who are acting stupidly would be acting immorally, why add the extra immoral part? If you say someone is acting stupidly, you're criticizing him already— meaning that if he could act a little more intelligently he would be "moral." So I don't understand adding the moral principle.

Because he regards self-interest as the only plausible "inviolable" principle and because self-interest is not a moral principle at all, he reaches his rejection of all moral principles through the assumption of inviolability as a necessary condition.

Nick is a Yale College senior planning to go to medical school. He views his values as "relative" because he cannot view them as "absolute." They are not "absolute," he says, because "a dilemma can be set up where two values are supposedly held highly and cannot be chosen between."

An "absolute" system, however, "should not involve any contradictions." He says of such conflicting values that pose dilemmas, "In terms of the absolute system, supposedly those shouldn't come up. The decision between them should be resolvable—the idea being that you shouldn't be able to create dilemmas."

In such an absolute system, "supposedly there would be no dilemmas as such." He explains, "All the values should be readily ranked so that as soon as you identify the salient points, then you can decide which way to go."

But "dilemmas" seem unavoidable. And "in the lack of such an ideal system [which would not be subject to dilemmas], the difference between all such systems that are in use does not really permit much of a moral judgment—I guess, in the strong sense of the word—to be placed on anybody."

He thus moves from the claim that his values conflict (in dilemmas) to the claim that his values, as a result, cannot be "absolute." And values that are not absolute, he believes, are "relative." Such values "do not really permit much of a moral judgment . . . to be placed on anybody."

Alan, a Cambridge graduate student, makes a similar argument. All values, he believes, are "ultimately relativistic in the sense that there is no absolute to which I can refer which will legitimate, guarantee, or confirm one's premises. Principles, however absolute they appear, may very often, given the proper context, clash—which to me undermines their absoluteness claims." This conflict, he explains, cannot be decided "with reference to principles because the principles, in clashing, are clearly not applicable." Alan, like Nick, believes that because principles clash they must be "ultimately relativistic."

Each of these reasoners argues that if morality does not consist in inviolable principles, then it must be subjective. Doug concludes that it would be impossible to capture the "tremendous complexity" of morality in "rigid laws"; but without rigid laws, he is left only with "arbitrary . . . rules of thumb." Jonathan concludes that without "absolute values which are inviolable" such as the Ten Commandments, he is left without any morality at all. Nick assumes, similarly, that "a moral judgment . . . in the strong sense of the word" requires values that are "absolute" in that they "should not involve any contradictions" or "dilemmas." The "moral systems" that do not live up to this "ideal," he concludes, "do not really permit much of a moral judgment." Last, Alan argues that when principles clash that "undermines their absoluteness claims"—justifying the view that they are "relativistic."

All these reasoners conclude that their moral positions cannot be "absolute" or objective and hence must be "subjective" or "arbitrary" because their principles cannot hold without exception. If only because the plurality of principles to which they are committed must, "given the proper context," as Alan says, conflict with one another, their principles cannot be exceptionless.[5] Each of these reasoners seems to be arguing from this notion of a necessary condition for an objectively valid or nonsubjective moral position:

> *Expectation 2*: An objectively valid moral position must consist in principles that hold without exception.

3.11. The Third Argument: Inevitable Indeterminacies

Doug adds another argument to the one in the last section. He begins by raising the question, once directed at conscientious

---

5. Exceptionless in the sense that we are never justified in acting contrary to the actions they prescribe.

objectors, "whether they would commit violence in order to keep their grandmothers from being raped":

> My reaction to that question is that it is not well defined. And in order to answer it properly if it were asked of me, I would have to say: Well, first of all, is my grandmother armed herself? Does she have any weapons herself? Does she mind being raped?
>
> These may perhaps sound funny, but in a more serious vein I might ask myself: What do I have to do to prevent her from being raped? Is it a question of closing the door? Is it a question of knocking the man down? Is it a question of shooting him in the arm? Is it a question of shooting him in the head? Is it a question of hacking up his body with an ax? Is there a policeman on the scene already? What do you exactly mean by rape? . . .
>
> And if he were to clarify the problem he could probably clarify it to a sufficient extent that I could answer, more or less ambiguously, that for the time being I can't think of any more information that I would like to ask, and in all cases I can imagine—conforming to the constraints you have given—that I would prevent my grandmother from being raped.

Yet Doug asserts that even this degree of assurance in his response to such a question is due to the fact that it is "an extreme problem." Even for such an apparently clear case

> there still comes a point where the posing of the problem becomes incredibly ambiguous—so much on the fringes of reality, so much on the fringes of understanding, so much on the fringes of judgment and interpretation, and so fuzzy, so ill-defined, so ambiguous that I could only give a somewhat ambiguous answer—for lack of an unambiguous understanding of exactly what the problem was.

The inevitability of such indeterminacies, Doug argues, undermines the sense in which anyone could plausibly claim to have a system of moral principles. He continues:

Now the way this relates to a set of moral principles is this: if someone was to design a set of moral principles, let's say Philosopher X, presumably, when he said that he had designed such a set of moral principles, he meant that I could give him a moral problem and he would be able to give me *an answer* based on those principles. My objection comes basically to this: I couldn't possibly state the problem. And in fact this is a fundamental objection. Moral decisions are inherently ambiguous decisions because moral problems are inherently ambiguous problems.

Because moral problems cannot be unambiguously defined, it is not possible, Doug believes, to devise a system that determines an answer to every moral question. But, Doug assumes, *if* someone were to devise a moral system, "presumably" this would mean that his system could determine an answer to any problem with which it was presented. This is his expectation about what a moral system would have to do to count as a moral system in any valid or objective sense.

Doug argues against such a system in another way: even if a complete moral system could be devised, it could not actually serve as a guide for human choice:

> Even if you believed that some God could set down a set of principles which would unambiguously and completely determine the proper moral decision in any situation . . . it would be so voluminous, so astronomically voluminous a system . . .

It would be so large and unwieldy a system, Doug concludes, that, "certainly if there were such a set of principles, it would not be small and no human or set of humans could possibly hold it in his mind at once. And if he could, he couldn't possibly spend the time to make such a decision. It would take him a trillion years to evaluate the moral principle properly." Complete principles are thus beyond reach—both because of the inherent ambiguity of the problems they would presume to resolve and because of the enormous complexity of a complete system were it to be devised.

Without a complete moral system that clearly determines answers to *any* problem, Doug concludes that we must be left with only "rules of thumb." "Instead of calling them [the 'imperfect' and incomplete considerations we are left with] moral laws or moral principles, we concede that the best thing that is possible is rules of thumb. . . . In the final analysis any set of principles which we design must be rules of thumb for social behavior." As we saw in the last section, Doug thinks of these rules of thumb as "arbitrary features" of his psychology. Without a complete system he has no "moral principles" or "moral laws" to which he attributes any validity.

Rob, a Yale biology student, explains that he does not have "an absolute sense of right and wrong." The reason is, "I'm constantly being presented with questions upon which I have no definitive opinion. If you were to ask me, 'Who's right in Ireland?' I don't know, man. I can't figure that one out. And, I suppose, people with a real absolute sense of right and wrong can figure that out. Fundamentalists, religious fundamentalists are among those who have the strongest sense of right and wrong."

When asked whether anybody can figure out these moral questions "in an absolute way" (to use his term), he replies:

> No, I don't think so. I don't believe there is any absolute right and wrong. Because if I did, then I would have been able to tell you what Heinz should have done. I don't have an absolute sense of right and wrong. I just have an internal sense of some sort of ethical conduct which is probably logically inconsistent.

For Rob, as for Doug, the incompleteness that he attributes to his moral position undermines its claim to absoluteness. The alternative to an "absolute" position, however, is a "subjective" one—which he admits "is probably logically inconsistent."

Nick also argues from the incompleteness and the indeterminacies of any moral system he can think of to the conclusion that these systems are subjective. His argument is based on the absence of a "perfect" system. "In the lack of such an ideal system . . . the difference between all such systems that are in use does not really permit much of a moral judgment, I guess, in the strong sense of the word."

When asked why he denies the possibility of such ideal or perfect systems, he explains that "one of the arguments was that the system should be able to handle all cases that you can think of." If he had such an "absolute" rather than a "relative" system, then the resolution of any problem would be predetermined: "the idea being, if you run across something new you immediately know exactly where it would fit in. . . . As soon as you decided that new question, you'd know exactly where to slip it in the hierarchy, whereas [in] the relative case the hierarchy is not quite as simple." In the relative case "it is not somehow predetermined completely by a previous system." He explains, "You still weigh them [values], but the decision can't essentially be determined ahead of time."

On the other hand, a defining characteristic of an "absolute" morality is that "such a system you could plug into, at all times, [and] you could come up with relatively easy answers."

Nick does not believe such an absolute, predetermined system is possible. But lacking such an absolute system, morality must be relative. Such a "nonideal" or "relative" system, he concludes, "does not really permit much of a moral judgment."

All these reasoners argue that in the absence of a moral system that determines an answer to any moral problem with which it is presented, their moral positions must be subjective. Doug, for example, assumes that if a "Philosopher X" were "to design a set of moral principles, then "presumably" that would mean that "I could give him a moral problem and he would be able to give me an answer based on those principles." Doug then argues from the complexity and ambiguity of moral principles that such a system—at least in any form that could actually guide human choice—is impossible. But without such a "perfect" system, he concludes that we must be left with only "rules of thumb," which he regards as "arbitrary."

Rob also argues that he lacks "an absolute sense of right and wrong," for he is "constantly being presented with questions" about which he has "no definitive opinion." As a result he must have merely a "subjective" sense of right and wrong.

In a similar way, Nick argues that if he had an "absolute" system he could "plug into" it at all times and "come up with relatively easy answers." But he cannot believe that morality is like that because there seem to be too many "dilemmas" and difficult choices that cannot be solved by a "predetermined" moral system. Hence he has to conclude that he can believe only in a "nonideal" or "relative" system. All these reasoners seem to be arguing from the following condition for an objectively valid or nonsubjective moral position, a necessary condition that their own positions cannot reasonably be construed as satisfying:

> *Expectation 3*: An objectively valid moral position must determine answers to *any* moral problem.

3.12. The Fourth Argument: Cosmic Neutrality

Doug explains the arbitrariness that he attributes to moral principles by proposing an analogy to the choices of a mathematician interested in developing a mathematical theory.

"To a mathematician, the choices of axioms from number theory that he wishes to use are arbitrary." He explains, "A pure theoretical mathematician's job is to examine the deductive consequences of axioms. He does not care . . . *qua* mathematician, he does not care what the axioms are. His interest is in developing the structure that follows from them, whatever they are, according to the logic which he allows himself to use. So the truth of axioms is arbitrary in the sense that the deductive process is always possible, no matter what axioms are used. (Even if they are inconsistent, the deductive process is possible, it just becomes instantly uninteresting.)"

According to Doug, the appropriate perspective for moral judgment is that of "someone who bears a relation to my moral universe similar to that which a mathematician bears to his axioms and the consequences from them." Such a person would be a kind of "external" moral judge—external in the complete neutrality he would bring to the problem. Just as "the mathematician is, in a sense, external to the system which he is investigating and the system which he is manipulating and making statements about, in that sense our external moral judge is external to my moral universe."

But when he completely "externalizes" himself, he has no basis for judgment at all. For he has abstracted himself from any basis even for taking an interest in human beings in the first place. "An external observer, one who doesn't distinguish a human being from a rock . . . would see a war between Nazis and non-Nazis as rocks colliding with one another." Doug explains, "That is to say that whatever principle he would use to decide his choice would have to be as arbitrary as some principle I might use to decide which of two rocks I would prefer to break."

From such a strictly neutral perspective, there would be no reason to value human beings at all. "I don't think there is anything fundamental, anything metaphysical, anything that in the final analysis can be said to be anything but arbitrary about the human species . . . its peculiar concepts of justice, wisdom, and right."

"In the whole scheme of the universe," Doug explains, "the question of whether the human race or any individual in it, or any other species, or the whole planet, or the whole galaxy lives or dies (or anything in between) doesn't matter at all." From this "external" perspective: "If the whole universe were to be destroyed tomorrow, that is not a moral question. If the sun should explode, the question of whether it has good or bad moral consequences doesn't make any sense."

"Their size in the scheme of the universe," he concludes about human beings, "is so minute, their consequences to the history of the universe are so inconsequential, as to be ludicrous." Within this picture of the universe as a whole, he can see no basis for preferring life to nonlife or human life to nonhuman life. From this perspective we are all "just patterns of energy and matter and flux and change." He contends, "It seems to me that it doesn't make sense to distinguish, in some fundamental way, a human being from the rock you are sitting on."

While admitting that in some ways "they are very different" and, in fact, "you can list for a million years ways in which they are different, profoundly different," Doug reasons that "you cannot argue from a list of differences that one is *better* than the other or that one deserves more consideration than the other in the scheme of the universe." Although it might be possible, for example, to arrive at a workable definition of life that would distinguish it from nonlife, there would still be no "external" fundamental basis for valuing life over nonlife because "it doesn't mark some physical or metaphysical distinction in the scheme of matter of the universe as a whole."

From this strictly neutral perspective, the choice of what Doug calls the "moral universe," that is, who is to be taken into account in a moral system, must be "arbitrary." "The choice of the set of men as a moral universe is arbitrary. It's just as legitimate to choose, let us say, the set of all life." He notes, for example, "I have read the works of American Indians where they claim to be extremely surprised by the actions of white men. That white men seem to feel that everything but white men is dead and available for the exploitation of white men." On the other hand, "the American Indians felt that everything was alive and that everything should be respected, and in particular the Indians felt a personal kinship with the trees and the animals."

"What I interpret that kind of statement to mean is that for the Indians the moral universe included more than just mankind; it included the animals, it included the trees, it included the land, it included the sun and the moon. For them, what was good for the sun and the moon was competitive with what was good for them."

In Doug's view, "The choice as to whether to include, to choose, the moral universe of men only, or to choose the moral universe of all living things, or to include rocks in that moral universe. . . . The decision of what the universe of moral choices is, what the universe of moral beings or morally relevant objects is . . . this choice is fundamentally arbitrary." In judging between different moral universes, "there seems to me to be no external criterion for judging the goodness of either moral system." He reasons, "Which society [that is, "universe"] is chosen is arbitrary . . . even whether you choose to include animals or not, or rocks or not, or whether you wish to include a morality at the cellular level rather than, in some sense, the species level of the biosphere. Which universe you choose is arbitrary."

Because the choices are arbitrary, from this perspective they are all "equally valid": "I recognize everyone else's goals in an intellectual, that is, in an externalized sense, I recognize any other individual's choice of moral universe as equally valid as my own . . . and his choice of goals for society as equally valid— judged by an external intelligence."

In his own case, he has chosen to include human beings and other animals that he can empathize with ("Me and everything like me is in my moral universe: things which aren't, aren't."). But this choice is not one that he believes to have any justification whatsoever. "The point is, my choice of moral universe is arbitrary and it's just what comes out of me. It's just what satisfies me. It's a product of my psychology, and if I were a different individual, if I had grown up different ways, if I had different fears, if I were not a human being at all but felt stronger kinship with animals or trees, I would choose a different one." "The only thing I can appeal to," he adds, "is the arbitrariness of the construction of my own psychology and my own anatomy. I can't give you a reason for that. I guess this is where the chain—the infinitely regressive chain of decisions in constructing my own moral framework—stops. The buck stops here. Saying that all such choices are arbitrary, I have made my choice."

At first, in describing this choice, he says, "It is the one that seems right to me." Then, correcting himself, he adds, "Not the one that seems right to me. The one that meshes best with all of the other components of my psychology. . . . It's the one that fits my personality."

This choice is based not on reasons but on "arbitrary" features of his "psychology": "I cannot argue with someone who chooses a larger universe. I can't argue with someone who chooses a smaller universe."

Similarly, the choice of "goals" in his moral universe (what those in it should aim to achieve) is also arbitrary. "The point is: the fact that the moral universe is applied to humans and other similar things doesn't give you any indication whatsoever as to what those goals should be. In fact, the use of the word *should* itself implies some external judgmental criterion, and the whole point I'm trying to make is that there are none of those."

Doug has goals in his personal moral system but they are "fundamentally indefensible":

> The choice of goals that I make are the ones consistent with my upbringing, my education, the humors circulating through my liver, spleen, and my brain, consistent with all the personality traits. . . . The goals that I have chosen for society and in terms of which I make moral decisions are fundamentally indefensible, beyond that level, and I just answer no more questions about them. I mean that I can pick all the holes in them that I want to, but in the final analysis I feel good this way.

He does not mind "picking holes" in his own personal judgments because he admits that they have no basis or validity. When he shifts from viewing moral problems from a kind of "external" perspective (where humans must be insignificant in any case) to viewing them from an "internal" one, he embraces his personal preferences as no more than the arbitrary products of his own psychology. Strictly speaking, when confronted with human moral problems, the only answer that he regards as intellectually defensible is: "I am *not* an external observer; I am an internal observer and it is *not fair for me to judge*. My criteria are not fundamental. They are relative to *my position* in the problem." As such, he can regard his criteria only as "rules of thumb" that he chooses "for convenience only" and that rest on nothing more than his own psychology.

Without an external basis—one that was independent of his own arbitrary interest in human beings, the earth, and life itself—his criteria are, he says, "not fundamental" but merely "relative to my position in the problem." There is no "defensible" basis whatsoever for him to value human beings over rocks or trees, no "defensible" basis for him to even value himself. From a strictly neutral perspective he sees no basis for choice at all. Once he completely externalizes himself, alternative possible moral positions all appear "equally valid."

Harvey, a student of mathematics, argues from a similar analogy in attempting to explain the "arbitrariness" that he attributes to moral judgment: "It's sort of like choosing the axioms for a system. Whereas the laws of logic—the deduction laws—are always absolute, you see? Choosing those axioms is a personalistic affair, but once you choose them, then the laws are absolute."

Just as there are no criteria for choosing the axioms for a system in the first place (it is a "personalistic affair"), there are no criteria for choosing values. They must be based, at bottom, on no more than "personal taste." "Trying to present foundations for morals and ethics on a broad enough level—unless it's tautology and unless it depends on formal rules of deduction . . . it won't go to the a priori axioms or the a priori foundation before any fact. It's all empty from that point of view. You can only have implicational or tautological statements about such things—just like in any system."

He has no basis, in the first place, for one set of assumptions rather than another. If he views them in the same way that he would view the axioms of a mathematical system, then they become, at bottom, entirely arbitrary. The only conclusions he can draw are "tautological." As he said above, "It's all empty from that point of view." Like Doug, once he abstracts himself from any personal view or reactions he might have, he finds that he has divorced himself from any basis for choosing one set of initial assumptions rather than another. As in a mathematical problem, he believes he must be neutral about such choices. This neutrality makes morality entirely a "personalistic affair."

Rob, a biology student, applies a similar kind of neutrality to the question of valuing human life in comparison with other forms of life. He sees no "fundamental" reason to value human beings more than any of the other unnumbered billions of species of life that have existed on earth.

He explains, in response to the Heinz dilemma: "I don't believe that human life, as such, is sacred and sacrosanct. I don't believe that the human species has an ultimate destiny or that it is distinct in any way at all from other organisms."

"In the context that I'm accustomed to thinking in, four and a half billion years of geological history and three and a half billion years of biological evolution . . . there have been estimates of anywhere from one to five *billion* species [that] have passed through the continuum during that period of time—of which mankind is *one* species out of unnumbered billions of species."

> And somehow to believe, or to maintain, that all that foregoing time, that vast amount of time, was really a preparatory note to the advent of "Homo" [that is, *Homo sapiens*]— for whom it was all made and who will, in his "infinite wisdom" turn it at last to its true and ultimate purpose— that's gotta be a pile of crap. That can't be justified by any but the most ethnocentric, egocentric, anthropocentric

mind. So I don't believe, in that context, I cannot believe, that mankind or the human species is or can be different, on any fundamental level, from any other organism.

Rob admits that, from this perspective, "I would have to completely deny all interest in humans other than my own pure intellect thinking about them—a distinct 'them.'" But when he looks upon the human race as just one species among others, the resulting moral position is "humanly inconceivable." He says, "In order for me to apply these things that I'm talking about, you have to completely neglect and negate such things as affection, love, responsibility, higher purpose." In other words, "In order to promote such a point of view, I would have to completely deny all emotional bonds to the human race."

These are the conclusions he comes to "as a pure intellect." "But me from the waist down, including my loins and my genitals and my stomach and my eyes and my heart, metaphysically speaking, cannot tolerate such a solution because it is inhumane, it is humanly inconceivable."

Hence if he were actually asked for help in the Heinz dilemma, or if he were asked for help by a stranger, "there's a bond that will develop between him and me—of just humanity, common humanity."

But these impulses toward compassion and humanity are, Rob believes, "rationally unsupportable" from his "cosmic perspective," that is, when he views human beings "in the context of all species." From this perspective he cannot believe that human life has value. To view it as "sacred and sacrosanct" would be an "anthropocentric" conclusion, that is, one biased toward human beings.

On the other hand, when he disconnects himself from human concerns, the resulting morality is "humanly inconceivable." He deals with this dilemma by clinging to his interest in other human beings and to his feelings of "common humanity"—but also by de-legitimating those feelings. He denies them validity because they appear "rationally unsupportable." "I don't *live* in the context of the cosmos," he says in describing the fractured viewpoint that results. "I just *think* in the context of the cosmos."

The strictly unbiased neutral perspective that Rob applies to the value of human life (compared with that of other species) is applied by Brian to the simpler problem of ethical disagreement with any other person:

> How can one say: "I don't have the revealed word of God, I don't know what is truth. I realize that *my reasons are exactly symmetrical with the other guy who I'm condemning, but somehow he's wrong and I'm right?*" I would like to see some argument for that, some consistent argument for that. And I don't see how one can even devise such an argument, just because of the nature of reason [italics added].

Here Brian is taking an "external" perspective—a neutral position between his own assumptions and those of anyone else he might be judging. But when he looks upon the disagreement in that way, he has no basis for resolving it—because he has abstracted himself from any assumptions that might be brought to bear upon the problem.

For Doug, just as a mathematician tries to be "external" to the problem he is investigating, an objective "moral judge" should try to be neutral between any preconceptions or initial assumptions. But once he "externalizes" himself in this way, he has no basis for judgment at all.

Harvey also attempts to step outside of any assumptions he might bring to moral problems. Just as there are no criteria for choosing the axioms for a system in the first place, he finds that there are no criteria for choosing ultimate values. When he attempts to view the problem completely "a priori" he finds that it is "all empty from that point of view." It becomes entirely a "personalistic affair."

Rob applies a similar kind of neutrality to the particular problem of the value of human life. Since there have been "unnumbered billions" of species of life on earth, to single out

Homo sapiens as the only one of value can only seem to him anthropocentric. To be objective he would have to look upon the human race as just one species among others. He would have to "completely deny all emotional bonds to the human race." Although he cannot accept the results of such a "cosmic" neutrality, his own personal morality—admittedly biased toward human beings—seems to him "rationally unsupportable."

All these reasoners appear to assume that an objective morality would have to be strictly neutral between alternative possible moral perspectives and initial assumptions. They could arrive at an objective position, they believe, only by somehow standing outside their own values and initial assumptions—and also those of anyone else. But as they abstract themselves in this way, they discover that they are left with no basis for choice at all.[6] These reasoners seem to be assuming that the following condition is necessary for an objective moral position:

> *Expectation 4*: An objectively valid moral position must be justifiable from the perspective of a strictly unbiased observer, that is, one who was completely neutral between alternative possible moral perspectives and initial assumptions.[7]

3.13. The Fifth Argument: The Demands of Conscience

Tom, a recent Yale graduate now teaching elementary school, finds it difficult to solve the dilemma of whether or not Heinz should steal the drug to save his wife's life. "If you asked the question," he begins, "Was he obligated to steal the drug— would anybody under those circumstances be obligated to steal the drug to save her life? I don't think that's the case." He explains, "I basically believe each person has to, I suppose, decide what he's got to do for himself. So you can't say [he] has a

6. For a similar point see Bernard Williams's discussion of the "midair" position in *Morality*, pp. 28–29.

7. This notion of a strictly unbiased observer should not be confused with the external (as opposed to internal) strategies of justification discussed below, in section 4.7.

moral obligation. . . . I guess I come down [to the position that] they should act with regard to their conscience, and I could say what I would hope that they would do, but not what they—I don't feel safe in saying what they're obligated to do."

The reason that he has difficulty in prescribing for others ("I'm not that clear on how other people should act") is that his basic claim that people should act with regard to their conscience renders morality quite variable and unpredictable.

In general, he says that people "are ultimately responsible to themselves and not to the society, or to the laws, or to what somebody else thinks. So that the druggist is ultimately responsible to what he really considers to be consistent with his conscience. And it might be what I'd consider to be worthless or useless or ridiculous." He adds, "Or what I would think would be immoral. But it wouldn't make it immoral for him. There's no absolute morality. Ultimately I think it has to come down to each individual accepting responsibility, deciding for himself."

By beginning with the fundamental notion that people should act in accordance with their "conscience," he is led to the conclusion that conflicting but conscientious moral opinions must be equally right. The druggist's moral decision might be what Tom regards as "immoral"—but it is still moral "for him" (the druggist).

Even in the case of Hitler, the most extreme case he can think of, Tom believes that "if it was consistent with his conscience then it would be valid, I suppose, for him to say 'Well, what I did was moral.'" However, Tom adds (judging from his own point of view), "But I would disagree with him."

If acts that agree with the "consciences" of those involved must all be "valid" or "moral" even though those judgments conflict, then, as Tom concludes, "There's no absolute morality." He says of his position, "Someone else could have different values—it's not an absolute." And without an absolute morality he is left with what he calls "just a value judgment."

These variable "value judgments" do not support consistent interpersonal conclusions. "There's no such thing as an 'act' *per se*, an abstract act being moral or immoral. You have to consider it with regard to someone." "That's the key thing," he continues. "No one is wise enough to be able to say flatly that an act is immoral or moral. You can decide for yourself, and you can try and persuade other people, but you have to leave with other people the responsibility of making up their own minds. I guess my morality is a morality of stupidity."

By believing that moral judgments must be consistent with the "consciences" of everyone, Tom is led to deny not only the objectivity of morality (the result is "just a value judgment") but also its universality (what is moral for one person is immoral for another who believes otherwise). The result is that he has no basis for condemning anyone who sincerely disagrees. Because "no one is wise enough" to make such a judgment, his morality is a "morality of stupidity."

Nancy, a Yale psychology major, also finds it difficult to judge others in the Heinz dilemma. For example, she refrains from condemning the druggist for refusing to sell the drug at a lower price because "I don't know what his moral system was." She explains, "According to my system I think he'd be wrong. According to his, maybe he was following his ethical system—in that case he's right . . . if he was going along with his convictions, then I guess he was right."

She admits that she strays from this position occasionally when she applies prescriptions to other people. "But they're not valid," she asserts. "I do go around saying he shouldn't have done that or something like that, but when you come down to it, unless I'm in that other person's head I don't have the right to condemn them or anything like that."

Like Tom, she begins with the notion that a judgment which departs from the "convictions" of those involved cannot be "valid" or correct. Yet these conscientious judgments lead to incompatible results ("according to my system I think he'd be wrong. According to his . . . he's right."). She cannot validly choose between such conflicting positions, she believes, provided they are sincerely held.

If someone disagrees with her, "I will condemn him but, I mean, it's not based on anything, and I have no right to condemn him—or my condemnation doesn't mean a thing—because that's my condemnation, it's based on my own feelings and my values, whatever they are . . . I mean I can't say objectively his aren't better than mine." Again, her assumption that judgments of "conviction" cannot be wrong leads her to question both the objectivity and the universality of morality.

In reacting to the same moral dilemma, Nick offers a similar argument. "The criteria for judging are always—always seem arbitrary," he begins. "Personally I would tend to prefer Heinz's position, but by that I can't overly condemn—or condemn period—anyone who might come up with other criteria, because that's personal."

"You can say that you personally feel, within your understanding of the problem, that the chosen values [those chosen by others] disagree with yours," he says in explaining the sense in which he can judge someone else. "And essentially, what it boils down to is to say, 'I wouldn't have solved the problem this way.' That would be it as far as you can say something is morally wrong."

He sees the "personal process" by which individuals arrive at moral views as immune—except on grounds of consistency—from criticism by others. "I may disagree with everybody else's opinion," he explains, "but I will have to respect it as being their opinion of the grounds on which they are acting." This means that "it is something that they arrived at by the same sort of personal process by which I arrived at my own decision." That, he explains, "renders them [the opinions] valid insofar as the decision is consistent with the grounds that are held by each person."

Nick cannot criticize anyone else's "personal" moral decisions. Because such personal deliberations—even when they conflict with his own (as in the case of the druggist)—must all be equally "valid," all these contrasting "moral criteria" have the same claim. However, because the resulting criteria are incompatible, he concludes that they must be "relative" or "arbitrary."

All these reasoners have argued that because conscientious moral decisions must be valid and immune from criticism, moral judgments must be arbitrary and relative. For when their assumption about conscientious moral decisions is combined with the inevitability of moral disagreement, the conclusion is inescapable that such conflicting conclusions cannot all be objectively correct. In this way an expectation about objectively valid moral positions once again leads to a subjectivist conclusion.

Tom, for example, argues from the assumption that everybody "should act with regard to their consciences" to the conclusion that "there's no absolute morality," and hence all he can offer is "just a value judgment." Nancy also argues from the assumption that anyone "going along with his convictions" must be right to the conclusion that she cannot settle moral disagreements objectively. Similarly, Nick argues from the assumption that all moral judgments in one's "moral makeup"—when they are arrived at by a "personal process" of sincere deliberation—must be "valid." But these personal judgments differ sufficiently that morality becomes "relative" to each individual decision, he concludes.

Each of these arguments proceeds from an assumption that the following condition is necessary for objectively valid moral positions:

> *Expectation 5*: An objectively valid moral position must be consistent with truly *conscientious* moral decisions (that is, those motivated only to determine what is morally right).

3.14. The Sixth Argument: Overwhelming Obligations

"I don't have an obligation to people," Brian insists. He is grappling with the question of how he should respond to the "little kids that walk around the Co-op" (soliciting donations).

He also mentions, "Somehow I feel I have a sympathy to the poor and hungry starving in India." But this sympathy does not correspond to any obligations he can accept. "When it came down to it," he admits, "I would say, of course, you help everybody. But not as a moral obligation. But just because it makes me feel good to help other people."

He explains why it is not a question of obligation. "Whatever argument I use to give to one, I have to give to another. And so I completely wipe out my own resources doing that. So I arbitrarily decide which ones I give to and which ones I don't. It doesn't seem to me that I have any real moral obligation—in principle—to help one. Because for me to fulfill that moral obligation, I wipe myself out. Because to help one means to help all. To help all means to wipe myself out."

If he gives in one case, "the question has certainly come up: then why don't you give to all sorts of other things?" His conclusion: "If you can't differentiate between, say, one cause and another good cause, then your obligation to them can't simply be based on the fact that they're good causes—because that would wipe you out."

The general problem is that "somehow principles applied to one little thing or another little thing seem very reasonable. But the arguments you have to reach that principle don't allow you to distinguish between applying that principle to the little circumstances or the big, unacceptable circumstances. And consequently you can't believe in the whole thing because you can't believe in the unacceptable circumstance."

Brian "can't believe in the whole thing" because he cannot believe that he would be obligated to wipe himself out. These individually reasonable obligations add up to an unacceptable total. But there seems to be no way of differentiating them. Every other human being—the little kids soliciting change at the Co-op, the starving in India—has an equivalent claim. The principles that would justify giving to one case would also justify giving to too many others. Because determining these obligations consistently—as he conceives them—would produce an overwhelming total, he refuses to accept the idea that he has any moral obligations at all.

David, an economics graduate student, grapples with the question of what Heinz should do if he does not love his wife. Should Heinz steal the drug to save his wife's life? "I think you could still make a case that the human life was worth more than protecting the property rights or the profit motives of the druggist," David responds. "Although, as soon as you start to make that move, you could then say, 'Well, what if it was the guy who lived down the block?'"

The difficulty he foresees is that "I'm less concerned about the lives of people I don't know at all than I am about people I do know well. That doesn't mean I'm not concerned. I am. But as soon as you start talking about people you don't know, the magnitude of the problem is so huge." He mentions the problem of starvation in far-off places such as Bangladesh: "You quickly get into a different scale of problem," he explains, "when you start considering it in the context of this parable of the lives of people you don't know at all. Because then you could save not only the guy down the street but the individual person in Bangladesh."

"This is a very difficult point," he adds, "a problem that unfortunately I feel forced to confront: I would have to ask myself how important it was to me to try and save this person's life [Heinz's wife]. And the reason I take it as a serious problem is because it's a specific example, but I think it's not unrelated to the question of how should I react to the imminent starvation of millions of people elsewhere in the world. How closely should I relate myself to that?"

His response is what he calls the "gravity theory—the idea being that things that are further away have less effect." He got this idea from a "prairie farmer" whose motto was "I just worry about what comes in front of me." But this gravity theory means that David cannot "consistently" value "human life." He explains, "The activist says, 'OK, you value human life and you want to be consistent, but you can't be concerned about everybody's life at once, because you'd just be immobilized, unable to act.' You can possibly do the gravity thing which says, 'Well, there are things closer to me that I should be concerned with first.' "

But in accepting the "gravity theory" he is not adopting what he regards as an "objective" moral position. "My position, as I've elaborated it, is not without contradictions. I am just making decisions for myself, given where I come from, or where I might be, depending on whose shoes I was standing in. And I cannot formulate a law that says everybody must behave this way."

David is not concerned with the inconsistencies in his position: "I don't believe there's such a thing as objective right—no such thing. I think really, it is determined by your own circumstances, your own attitudes, in the way you draw the line personally, at the kinds of activities you actively or passively support or reject." "I make moral decisions for myself," he adds. "I haven't judged other people because I think their circumstances differ."

While he says, "It would be nice to be able to retreat, in a sense, to a belief in objective moral principles," he feels he cannot. "I don't feel I have made the moral commitment, or I have the sufficient moral basis to prescribe for other people."

A similar argument arises when Jonathan brings up the question whether he is obligated to help the "starving in India." "It seems to me that because it's difficult to draw the line of how much to give away, giving anything away is hypocritical. . . . It seems that if someone says, 'I give a hundred dollars every year to CARE,' and I say, 'Oh, a hundred dollars? Why not a hundred and one?' And they say, 'OK, you make it a hundred and one, I'll give a hundred and one.' And I'll say, 'Well, why not a hundred and two?' And it'll go on like that."

"And eventually there's going to be one point where they're gonna stop," Jonathan concludes. "Let's say we stop at $200. And I'll say, 'You think your 201st dollar is going to be more important to *you* than to that person starving in India?' And he'll say, 'Well, I don't know.' And I'll say, 'Well, what about the 198th dollar? Evidently you think that was helping the person in India.'"

"And so it's going to lead to a difficult position," says Jonathan. "If you give anything at all, you're going to have to draw the line somewhere." The difficulty Jonathan foresees in "drawing the line" is that the "altruist" must either be "hypocritical" or he must make so many sacrifices that he himself will risk starving.

"I think the altruist, by giving one hundred dollars and not more, is hypocritical," he explains. "He'd have to give *all* his money away until he was the poorest person on the earth." "Because, if he was altruistic," Jonathan continues, "and he really cared about the welfare of others more than he cared about himself, then he would give it all away. And he would give away the 201st as well as the 200th, and the 202nd and the 203rd—everything, until he gave so much away that he was as poor as the poorest person—which he obviously wouldn't do."

Jonathan says he respects anyone who would go to the limits that a consistent "altruism" would require, but he cannot require it of himself. He mentions Gandhi, for example, "whose entire possessions were a pair of glasses and a bowl, some sandals and a robe, I think. Now he could unhypocritically say that he didn't believe in materialism, or that he was altruistic. But I think you have to go to that extreme."

"I would respect Gandhi saying 'I am altruistic,'" he adds, "as opposed to Joe Blow who lives in a house and has a washing machine and gives money to CARE."

"Joe Blow," Jonathan explains, "is doing one of two things. He either *thinks* he's altruistic and really isn't—and is being hypocritical—or else he is getting a certain estimated dollar value, a quantifiable pleasure, out of it. Because dollars given have a value also—because it's a pleasure helping other people."

In the latter case the motivation for giving is not "obligation" but "pleasure." It is no longer altruism in the moral sense but rather an action undertaken for personal satisfaction. This kind of giving conforms, in fact, to Jonathan's explicitly egoistic position. He gives to charities, on occasion, but "I wouldn't give anything to some place like CARE because I'd never understand what's happening . . . there'd be much more reason to give money, charity, to a local organization for a specific effect."

The concern of such giving, however, would be pleasure to the donor rather than good effects to the recipient. It is not giving for the sake of principle but rather giving so that the donor can experience satisfaction from it. Jonathan can endorse that kind of giving—but on self-interested rather than on moral grounds.

According to Jonathan, the moral altruist must either be hypocritical or he must be willing to apply his principles consistently. If he applies them consistently to each dollar, in turn, he would have to give up "everything, until he gave so much that he was as poor as the poorest person." Rather than be drawn down what he calls this "slippery slope," Jonathan avoids considering the problem in moral terms at all.

Each of these reasoners has argued that an objectively valid moral position, if applied consistently, would produce obligations so demanding that they are beyond what can be accepted or believed in. In each case, the argument is based on the notion that moral obligations must be determined with what might be called *strict impartiality*, that is, with no special regard for one's own interests, situation, or relations with others. The underlying premise is that the interests of strangers must be considered precisely as one's own, or one's family's.

Hence David interprets his admission that he is "less concerned about the lives of people I don't know at all than I am about people I do know well" as incompatible with "objective right." In turning to a "gravity theory"—which commits him to take special account of those close to him—he believes he is abandoning an objective moral position.

Brian also refuses to admit "a real moral obligation" to help in even one case. "Because for me to fulfill that moral obligation, I wipe myself out. Because to help one means to help all. To help all means to wipe myself out." To determine obligations in a way that gives strictly impartial consideration to everyone would determine an overwhelming total of obligations—a conclusion he cannot accept: "You can't believe in the whole thing [morality] because you can't believe in the unacceptable circumstances" [the overwhelming total of obligations].

Jonathan argues, step by step, to a similar conclusion. A moral "altruist" would have to give others at least the consideration he gave himself. But if such an altruist stopped short after giving, say $200, he would be forced to admit that the 201st dollar would also do others more good than it would do himself. A "real" moral altruist would have to give until he was "as poor as the poorest person in the world." Anything less than that would be "hypocrisy." But Jonathan finds the total demands of the nonhypocritical alternative enormously implausible.

The argument is thus that an objective moral position— because its obligations would have to be determined with strict impartiality—must also produce overwhelmingly demanding obligations. Because these reasoners cannot believe in, or accept, such obligations, they make no claim to such an objective moral position.

There is ambiguity in these accounts about what would constitute obligations that are too demanding. Implicitly, these reasoners assume that there is some limit to the amount of sacrifice that can be demanded of them—as a matter of obligation or moral requirement. As in the standard philosophical distinction between obligation and supererogation, they assume some point where sacrifice is so great as to be heroic or "beyond the call of duty." These reasoners are simply assuming some such upper limit (short of physical impossibility). They are unable to accept that morality would require such great sacrifices as a matter of obligation. Yet the obligations that would appear morally plausible—and non-hypocritical— would cumulatively require sacrifices clearly on this scale. This is how they are led to the point where, in Brian's words, they "can't believe in the whole thing."

The assumption about an objective morality from which these arguments proceed can be stated thus:

Expectation 6: An objectively valid moral position must determine obligations with *strict impartiality*, that is, it must determine obligations with no special regard for the agent's interests, situation, or relations with others.

4. Ethical Foundations and Liberal Theory

4.1. The General Pattern of Argument

The arguments for subjectivism canvassed in the last chapter share a common structure. Each argument proceeds from the lack of an assumed necessary condition for an objective moral position. This lack of the proposed necessary condition might be construed in various ways that are not clearly distinguished in the interviews. First, it might be construed merely as a claim about the reasoner's own moral position. Let us term this the *position-specific* construction of the argument. Second, it might be construed as a claim about any possible moral position. Let us term this the *general impossibility* construction of the argument.

If nonfulfillment of the assumed necessary condition is interpreted merely in the position-specific sense—merely as a claim about the reasoner's own moral position—then the arguments are complete largely in the form presented. The reasoners are self-conscious and explicit about the absence of the proposed necessary conditions as any claim they could reasonably make on behalf of their own moral positions. As a result, their route to subjectivism is straightforward:

1. An objectively valid moral position must have characteristic X (specified by one of the six expectations already discussed).

2. My position lacks characteristic X.
3. Therefore, my position cannot be objectively valid (and, hence, must be "subjective" or "arbitrary").

This route to subjectivism is clear. When directed at the reasoner's own position the argument is, obviously, logically valid. Whether it is sound (whether it is a valid argument proceeding from true premises) depends, crucially, on step 1 above, the assumption that an objectively valid position must have the stated necessary characteristics defined by one or another of the six expectations. For each argument, if we can plausibly avoid construing objective validity so as to require the stated characteristic X, we can avoid the conclusion (step 3) that the moral position in question must be subjective. My efforts to show the avoidability of subjectivism will hinge on this strategy.

Some subjectivist reasoners, however, appear to interpret their conclusions more broadly. They seem to attribute subjectivism not merely to their own moral positions but to all possible moral positions that are plausible or credible. Any credible moral position that anyone might formulate is, inevitably or necessarily, subjective or arbitrary, they seem to conclude. This broader pattern of inference takes roughly this form:

1. An objectively valid moral position must have characteristic X (specified by one of the six expectations).
2. All possible moral positions that are credible lack characteristic X.
3. Therefore, all possible moral positions that are credible cannot be objectively valid (and, hence, must be "subjective" or "arbitrary").

In this version the basis for step 2 is at least as controversial as the basis for step 1. In the simple, position-specific version of the argument, the reasoner's own construction of his position could be presumed, largely, to settle the question whether that position had characteristic X. But the general impossibility version is much broader, since it applies to any credible position that anyone might formulate, including ones that no one has yet invented.

By "credible" in step 2 above, I mean plausible or believable. In many cases it might be possible for a reasoner to construe a position that satisfied one or another of the expectations (say, that it held without exceptions or that it resolved any moral question), but the moral prescriptions required for the position to satisfy the expectation might not be ones in which the reasoner could believe. Recall Jonathan's discussion of "not stealing" as a principle, progressively reformulated for further exceptions. The exceptions are necessary for moral, not logical, reasons. We could logically hold to the position, for example, that stealing is never permitted, but we would then be saddled with unattractive implications for the case of Heinz, who would be required to stand by idly while his wife died.

The argument seems to be that although there are possible moral positions that might be formulated so as to conform to the expectations, these positions have particular moral implications that the reasoner cannot find credible on moral grounds. At first sight it may seem strange that these reasoners are employing something like a notion of moral credibility while at the same time concluding that moral opinions are entirely subjective or arbitrary (and, hence, that any moral opinion is, in a sense, as good as any other). However, their strategy might be defended as one in which they reason that *if* there were any such thing as a credible moral position, it would have certain specifiable implications; those implications include lack of characteristic X (required for objective validity); therefore no credible moral position can be objectively valid (and therefore, in a sense, there can be no such thing as a credible moral position).

Even construed in this way, however, there is a considerable gap in the inferences supporting step 2 in the ambitious, general impossibility version of the argument. The fact that the reasoners are not now aware of any credible moral position that has the stated characteristic does not, in itself, yield the conclusion that no *possible* moral position they would regard as credible could have the stated characteristic. As Jonathan, for example, envisions further exceptions to his rule about not stealing, perhaps he might eventually arrive at a position whose implications he could subscribe to for every case, without any further exceptions or qualifications. We do not know whether or not a credible version of any given principle might be invented in the future, since the process of reformulation can always be continued. The number of principles no one has yet invented is open-ended and can always be added to. In other words, for any of the characteristics specified by the six expectations, it is always possible that some new formulation of a moral position, now unanticipated by the reasoner, could be invented so as to conform to the stated expectation.

Consider a third possible construction of the argument, less ambitious than the general impossibility claim but more ambitious than the position-specific version. It might be summarized as:

1. An objectively valid moral position must have characteristic X (specified by one of the six expectations).
2. Any credible moral position I can reasonably expect to arrive at lacks characteristic X.
3. Therefore, any credible moral position I can reasonably expect to arrive at cannot be objectively valid (and, hence, must be "subjective" or "arbitrary").

Let us call this third version the *reasonable expectations* construction of the argument. Sympathetically interpreted, its general structure comes closest, I believe, to the spirit of the arguments for subjectivism already discussed. Our subjectivist reasoners clearly wish to offer more than autobiographical reports about their own personal positions. But their arguments also fall short of anything as grand as the general impossibility construction. In the next sections I will attempt to bolster and supplement this third construction of the route to subjectivism by offering similar arguments in the same spirit. These arguments should have the effect of strengthening step 2 in the construction. Then, once we have as forceful a version as we can arrive at of this pattern of argument, I will present a strategy for counteracting it. This strategy will hinge on denying step 1 by attempting to *disconnect* the account of objective validity from each of the proposed expectations. If successful, this would obviously block the inference to subjectivism in step 3. Although this strategy does not decisively defeat or refute subjectivism, it does defuse these arguments by demonstrating how the apparently irresistible conclusion can be avoided. And it will have done so for the *strongest* version of the subjectivist arguments we will have succeeded in formulating.

The six expectations employed by our subjectivist reasoners are not random assumptions. They have a certain coherence which is most easily glimpsed by attempting to envision the position that would result if all six expectations were satisfied. Because of expectations 1 and 2 (that principles be rationally unquestionable and that they hold without exception), this position would obviously constitute a form of absolutism (position I in our scheme of classification). It is, in fact, a particularly demanding form that found its most influential philosophical expression in Kant's notion of the Categorical Imperative. In citing Kant I mean only to point to a systematic example of the position, one that has had a great influence on the development of our common moral culture (and one that was influenced by it as well). However, I do not mean to imply that our ordinary reasoners had Kant specifically in mind when they employed these assumptions.[1]

Kant offers an account of morality based on the rational moral law—the Categorical Imperative—which conforms to all six expectations:

1. As he explains in the *Groundwork*:

All moral concepts have their seat and origin in reason completely *a priori*, and indeed in the most ordinary human

---

1. Kant, of course, claimed that his starting point was nothing more than "ordinary rational knowledge of morality." See Kant, *Groundwork*, p. 60.

reason just as much as in the most highly speculative: they cannot be abstracted from any empirical, and therefore merely contingent, knowledge.[2]

We know these moral judgments with "apodeictic" certainty. They are rationally unquestionable in the sense of our first expectation.

2. Moral judgments hold "with strict universality, that is, in such a manner that no exception is allowed as possible."[3] From the very notion of a moral "law" Kant derives the requirement of our second expectation, that principles be inviolable.

3. The Categorical Imperative serves as a "compass"[4] for the resolution of all moral questions. The moral law, Kant believes, is always sufficient to determine the will to do what is objectively right—if only we choose to act from duty alone. His position thus includes the claim of our third expectation—that the Categorical Imperative determines answers to *any* moral question.

4. The Categorical Imperative is the moral law valid from the "point of view" of "noumenal" selves who are entirely independent of the causally determined world of phenomena of which we are ordinarily aware. This is "a point of view which reason finds itself constrained to adopt outside appearances in

2. Ibid., p. 79.
3. Immanuel Kant, *Critique of Pure Reason*, translated by Norman Kemp Smith (London: Macmillan, 1929), p. 44. Consider these examples of Kant holding to principles without exception:

> The duty of veracity . . . is an unconditional duty which holds in all circumstances.

> To be truthful in all declarations is therefore a sacred unconditional command of reason, and not to be limited by any expediency.

(Immanuel Kant, "On a Supposed Right to Tell Lies from Benevolent Motives," in *Kant's Theory of Ethics*, translated by T. K. Abbot [London: Longman's Green, 1909] pp. 363–64.)
Acton criticizes Kant for this kind of "rigorism." See H. B. Acton, *Kant's Moral Philosophy* (London: Macmillan, 1970), pp. 64–65.
4. From Kant, *Groundwork*, cited in Acton, p. 15.

order to conceive itself as practical"[5] (that is, in order to conceive itself as subject to morality or practical reason). We can "think" ourselves into this standpoint, but we cannot "intuit" or "feel" ourselves into it.[6] This "noumenal" standpoint resembles the strictly neutral perspective that our ordinary reasoners were envisioning in the fourth argument.

5. If we "will" an action from "duty" alone, then according to Kant it must be valid for all rational beings. Hence, all "conscientious" moral decisions—those determined by duty alone—fulfill our fifth expectation.

6. According to the moral law, every other rational being must be treated as an "end in itself." This will not come about "unless everyone endeavours also, so far as in him lies, to further the ends of others. For the ends of a subject who is an end in himself must, if this conception is to have its *full* effect in me, be also, as far as possible, *my* ends."[7] [italics in original]. A moral agent in a "Kingdom of Ends" is to regard the ends of every other rational being in precisely the way he regards his own. Such a morality is, in the sense of our sixth expectation, "impartial."

Kant offers this account of the Categorical Imperative, furthermore, as a necessary condition for any attribution of objective validity to morality. As he says near the end of the *Groundwork*, "Anyone, therefore, who takes morality to be something and not merely a Chimerical Idea without truth, must at the same time admit the principles we have put forth."[8]

Each of our subjective reasoners has rejected one part or another of this picture of an objective morality. And as a result each has concluded, in effect, that morality must be "merely a Chimerical Idea without truth." It is in this sense that subjectivism can be interpreted as the residue left over from a failed Kantianism.

5. Kant, *Groundwork*, p. 126.
6. Ibid.
7. Kant, *Groundwork*, p. 98. See the discussion of strict impartiality in sections 3.15 above, and 4.4 and 4.5 below.
8. Kant, *Groundwork*, p. 112.

But why is the full version of this kind of Kantian absolutism difficult to maintain? In the sections that follow I will attempt to bolster the six arguments of our ordinary reasoners under three headings: (a) the jurisdiction problem for arguments 1, 4, and 5; (b) the foreseeability problem for arguments 2 and 3; and (c) the overload problem for argument 6. After the basic thrust of their arguments has been extended and strengthened, I will show how subjectivism may nevertheless be avoided—provided that we are willing to relinquish absolutist expectations.

4.2. The Jurisdiction Problem

In the first argument our reasoners found that every moral assumption was open to further question and that such chains of questioning were not susceptible to a "stopping point." In the absence of "moral revelation" or the substantive "question that was self-answering," their most fundamental premises simply had to be assumed at some point without any further rationale or justification. In following the "infinite regress" that their demand for justification opened up, they reached a point where they could only say "just because" in support of their most fundamental assumptions.

The fourth argument is closely related. A truly objective morality, our reasoners argue, would have to be justifiable from a strictly unbiased position—one that was completely neutral between alternative possible moral perspectives and initial assumptions. They must somehow completely abstract from their own biases and concerns, and those of anyone else. But when they "externalize" themselves in this way, they find that they have no basis for choice at all.

The fifth argument proceeds from the assumption that truly conscientious moral decisions must be objectively valid. But when this assumption is combined with the facts of moral disagreement—that equally conscientious moral decisions sometimes support incompatible conclusions—a unified objective morality (applied universalizably to everyone) becomes impossible.

Kant, of course, contended that the "rational moral will" within each of us operated so as to satisfy these expectations. We could know it with apodeictic certainty (satisfying expectation 1); it was valid for all rational beings viewed from the perspective of "noumenal selves" (satisfying expectation 4); and it would lead all truly conscientious persons to moral agreement (satisfying expectation 5).

Yet our subjectivist reasoners can (and do) deny, with logical consistency, that they are endowed with a rational moral will that has such properties. How might a defender of the Kantian-absolutist position (or any other position claiming to satisfy these expectations) respond?

Kant's famous response, developed most forcefully in the *Groundwork*, was to tie his account of the moral will (determined by the rational moral law, the Categorical Imperative) to the possibility of autonomy or freedom. Either human beings (and indeed rational beings more generally) are subject to the moral law as he describes it, or their actions must be determined "heteronomously" by the empirical operation of causal necessity rather than "autonomously" through the operation of the moral law.

It should be obvious that our subjectivist reasoners can respond to this move in the debate without altering their positions. They need not claim "freedom" or "autonomy" in the Kantian sense. First, it would not undermine their subjectivist moral positions were they to avoid claiming freedom or autonomy in any sense, that is, were they to accept an entirely deterministic account of their actions. Second, they could assert freedom or autonomy in some sense other than the Kantian one, in some sense that does not equate it with action determined by the *moral* law. Kant does not claim to have proved that morality necessarily applies to human action, only that *if* freedom or autonomy is possible, it is necessarily through action defined by the moral law in the sense he proposes.[9] Hence, even if our reasoners were to accept Kant's account of freedom and autonomy as unproblematic,[10] they could maintain their positions by accepting the charge of "heteronomy" (lack of "autonomy").

It may be worth pausing to consider a recent variant of the Kantian argument, one developed with special rigor and sophistication. Alan Gewirth, in his influential *Reason and Morality*, offers a defense of the objectivity of morality based on the possibility of human action. Unlike the original Kantian argument, free human action in Gewirth's account is not simply equated with the operation of the moral law. Rather, it is defined explicitly in nonmoral terms so as to apply to any human actor. Gewirth argues that it is not logically open to any human actor, including "nihilists" and "amoralists," to deny the foundation for morality he proposes.

Gewirth's general strategy is succinctly summarized in this passage:

> Every agent must claim, at least implicitly, that he has rights to freedom and well-being for the sufficient reasons that he is a prospective purposive agent. From the content of this claim it follows, by the principle of universalizability, that all prospective purposive agents have rights to freedom and well-being. If the agent denies this generalization, he contradicts himself. For then he would be in the position of both affirming and denying that being a prospective purposive agent is a sufficient condition of having rights to freedom and well-being.[11]

The crucial issue for our purposes is the sense in which a person, if he is to be a prospective purposive agent, must affirm, if only "implicitly," that he has "rights to freedom and well-

9. See, for example, the quotation identified by n. 8 above.

10. See Jonathan Bennett, *Kant's Dialectic* (Cambridge: Cambridge University Press, 1974), chap. 10.

11. Alan Gewirth, *Reason and Morality* (Chicago: University of Chicago Press, 1978), p. 133.

being." After that point the argument is relatively straight-forward: if I assert that I have rights to freedom and well-being on the sufficient grounds that I am a prospective purposive agent, then I must also grant that other such agents have a sufficient basis for the same rights.

However, note the gap between an agent's claim that freedom and well-being are good or desirable (that they are goods necessary for his prospective purposive action) and that he has a "right" to them.[12] Gewirth's claim is that "the agent's statement, 'My freedom and well-being are necessary goods,' entails his further statement, 'I have rights to freedom and well-being.'"[13] But Gewirth admits that the latter statement adds something to the former:

> Between the agent's statement that his freedom and well-being are necessary goods and his further statement or claim that he has rights to these goods, there are the important differences that in the latter statement the goods are set forth not merely as valuable or desirable but as objects to which the agent is entitled or which he ought to have as his due, and the agent is in the position not only of valuer or evaluator but also of claimant. The claim-making may be only implicit or dispositional, a matter of attitude, of how the agent regards himself in relation to other persons; but in any case he here lays claim to freedom and well-being as goods to which he is entitled—which are due him. It is this entitlement that directly constitutes the nature of the rights he claims for himself.[14]

The problem is that an agent may grant that his own freedom and well-being are necessary goods in the instrumental sense that they define necessary conditions for his functioning as an agent, without any requirement that he add a claim that

---

12. See, for example, the review by Adina Schwartz in *The Philosophical Review* (October 1979), pp. 654–56, and the criticisms in Alasdair MacIntyre's *After Virtue* (Notre Dame: University of Notre Dame Press, 1981), pp. 64–65.

13. Gewirth, *Reason and Morality*, p. 64.

14. Ibid., pp. 64–65.

they are "due" him or that he is "entitled" to them. Although, as Gewirth argues, there is a sense in which " 'I do X for purpose E' entails 'E is good,' "[15] and although this notion of "good" may be applied, as Gewirth proposes, to the "generic" features of action such as "freedom and well-being,"[16] this notion of good implies only "a favorable or positive evaluation of the objects or purposes to which it is attributed."[17] It does not entail that the objects or goods that are positively evaluated be claimed as entitlements or as due to the agent.

Although Gewirth is correct that an "amoralist," in order to be an "agent" in his sense, would have to approve, in some sense, of his own freedom and well-being,[18] such an amoralist would not be committed by that approval to any claim that he was "entitled" to that freedom and well-being or that it was "due" him. Our subjectivist reasoners, who interpret any moral claims they happen to employ in terms of likes, tastes, or preferences, could all describe their approval of their own freedom and well-being (because it is necessary for their functioning as agents) without laying claim to entitlements. Following their comparison of moral tastes to their tastes for food, they might assert that they like their own freedom and well-being just as they like chocolate ice cream, without asserting that others owe them noninterference with their freedom or well-being—any more than others owe them noninterference with their consumption of chocolate ice cream.

Furthermore, even if we were to accept Gewirth's claim that this positive attitude can be inferred to apply universally to all (prospective purposive) agents, unlike the taste for chocolate ice cream, the universality of the attitude, by itself, does nothing to bridge the gap between things that are "good" merely in the sense that they are approved of, and things that are "goods" in the sense that one is entitled to, or owed, them.

15. Ibid., p. 49.
16. Ibid., p. 52.
17. Ibid., p. 51.
18. Ibid., p. 95.

The Kantian argument from autonomy—and Gewirth's elaborate variation based on the generic features of human action—illustrate the extensive room for maneuver available to our subjectivist reasoners. They can assert that they are free or autonomous in many senses that fall short of a Kantian commitment to the moral law. Furthermore, they can admit that their own freedom and well-being are, in some sense, necessary for their functioning as human agents; and they can affirm, as a result, that they have a positive attitude toward their own freedom and well-being. This latter admission, however, does not commit them to a "rights" claim that must be universalizable to other persons. Just as they have a positive attitude toward their own freedom and well-being, they may grant that others have a similar attitude toward their own (respective) freedom and well-being—without any entitlements or moral requirements following for either party. Hence, subjectivists can affirm their character as human agents without also committing themselves either to Kantian "autonomy" or to "rights" to the generic features of action, as Gewirth claims.

I have paused to look in detail at Gewirth's argument because it is unusual among sophisticated modern efforts precisely because it attempts to deny this room for maneuver—in order to provide a foundation for morality that even the amoralist and the nihilist must grant. By contrast, the distinctive strategy in the recent development of liberal political theory has been the refinement of moral decision procedures which, while Kantian in certain key respects, make a less ambitious claim than that made by the full Kantian absolutist position (or by Gewirth in the argument above). These new moral decision procedures are less ambitious in that they grant, explicitly, that "egoists," "amoralists," and others who deny the "moral point of view" in one way or another may, with logical consistency, avoid committing themselves to the jurisdiction of these procedures.

The moral decision procedures in recent political theory, like the positions discussed by our ordinary reasoners, cannot plausibly live up to the absolutist expectations whose nonfulfillment provides the basis for subjectivism. After establishing that claim here I will show, in section 4.5, how these procedures can, despite all their limitations, provide a strategy for moving beyond subjective morality. That strategy will depend on a careful consideration of the full range of objective and subjective alternatives provided by our scheme of seven ethical positions.

The recent resurgence in liberal political theory has been fueled by a distinctive development—the definition of appropriate moral perspectives or decision procedures for the selection of principles that are to have priority in a liberal state, at least under ideal conditions. Rawls's "original position,"[19] Ackerman's notion of "neutral dialogue,"[20] Dworkin's notion of "equal concern and respect,"[21] and the perfectly sympathetic spectator of the classical utilitarians (an argument recently reformulated by Peter Singer)[22] all have this character. They define a perspective of *impartiality for the equal consideration of relevant claims or interests*, and this perspective is offered as the foundation for social choice in a just society (or at least in the liberal version of a just society). Some of these decision procedures also extend to individual choice, but these extensions have sometimes proved controversial.[23]

It is worth pausing for a moment to consider how these procedures differ. Rawls's theory, probably the most influential

19. Rawls, *A Theory of Justice*, pp. 17–22.

20. Ackerman, *Social Justice in the Liberal State*, p. 11.

21. Ronald Dworkin, *Taking Rights Seriously* (Cambridge, Mass.: Harvard University Press, 1978), pp. 234–38, 275–78. For an illuminating discussion of Dworkin's general strategy see H. L. A. Hart, "Between Utility and Rights," in Alan Ryan, ed., *The Idea of Freedom* (Oxford: Oxford University Press, 1979), pp. 77–98.

22. The classic discussion of the perfectly sympathetic spectator can be found in Adam Smith, *The Theory of Moral Sentiments* (Indianapolis: Liberty Classics, 1969), pp. 22, 31, 33, 35–38, 41, 71, 161–62, 271, 247–49. For recent discussions see Rawls, *A Theory of Justice*, pp. 183–92, and Peter Singer, *Practical Ethics*, chap. 1.

23. See Fishkin, *The Limits of Obligation*, parts 1 and 3, for a critique of such efforts.

example of this strategy, would have us imagine ourselves choosing principles of justice from behind a "veil of ignorance," deprived of all particular knowledge of ourselves or of our society. We are to choose principles of justice out of self-interest under conditions that permit us to know nothing in particular about ourselves, nothing that distinguishes us from anyone else. Forced to choose in the interests of anyone, we cannot design principles so as to favor ourselves. The root notion, Rawls notes, is similar to the familiar "cut and choose" procedure for cutting a cake fairly.[24] Just as the person cutting a cake does not know which slice will be left for him (if he follows the procedure of letting the others choose first), the agent in the original position does not know which position will turn out to be his. In both cases, self-interest can be harnessed via control over information to lead to fair results. In some ways, however, the analogy is imperfect, since the cake cutter knows both the number of slices and that the worst piece will be left for him. Both of these factors are left indeterminate in Rawls's original position, although Rawls argues, controversially, that such an agent will, nevertheless, choose principles as if his "enemy" were to "assign him his place."[25] Hence he must be rationally interested in maximizing the minimum share.

Superficially, Ackerman's notion of "neutral dialogue" seems quite different. Instead of being deprived of all particular information, Ackerman's imaginary participants are equipped with something approaching omniscience. Principles are arrived at under a "perfect technology of justice"—a kind of science fiction situation where "there never is any practical difficulty in implementing the substantive conclusions of a neutral dialogue."[26]

24. Rawls, *A Theory of Justice*, p. 85.
25. Ibid., p. 152. For a critique of this claim see Fishkin, "Justice and Rationality: Some Objections to the Central Argument in Rawls's Theory," *American Political Science Review* 69, no. 2 (June 1975): 615–29.
26. Ackerman, *Social Justice in the Liberal State*, p. 21.

However, the requirement that the dialogue be "neutral" yields a condition of impartiality or equal consideration of claims that fills the same role in Ackerman's theory that the "veil of ignorance" does in Rawls's theory. Ackerman's notion of "neutrality" is that

> no reason is a good reason if it requires the powerholder to assert: (a) that his conception of the good is better than that asserted by any of his fellow citizens, *or* (b) that, regardless of his conception of the good, he is intrinsically superior to one or more of his fellow citizens.[27]

This notion of neutrality specifies a kind of impartiality, since it rules out arguments that would give more than equal consideration to any person's conception of the good or that would give any person more than equal consideration *per se* (consider any person "intrinsically superior"). The neutrality condition operates as a barrier to conversations that would wrongly legitimate a particular distributional structure. This barrier (along with two less important conditions)[28] filters out all proposals, Ackerman argues, except a version of equality he entitles "undominated diversity." Although neutrality rules out any claims of superiority, it ends up permitting a series of inferences along the lines of, "I'm at least as good as you are, therefore, I should get at least as much."[29]

Another moral decision procedure with wide currency in liberal political theory is the perfectly sympathetic spectator of classical utilitarianism. Going back to Adam Smith, this idea would have us imagine a spectator who reproduced in himself every pain and pleasure in the world. Perfectly reproducing in himself every sensation of disutility and utility experienced by

27. Ibid., p. 11.
28. In addition to the neutrality condition, Ackerman stipulates "rationality" (requiring that reasons be given) and "consistency," *Social Justice in the Liberal State*, pp. 4–7.
29. Ibid., section 14.

anyone, he would prefer those states of the world that maximized the overall balance of pleasure over pain. In this procedure another account of impartiality (namely, perfectly sympathizing with everyone's pain and pleasure in the same way) is combined with an account of everyone's interests (namely, utility) so as to yield the familiar principle of aggregate utility.[30]

Peter Singer, in his recent attempts to rehabilitate and defend a form of utilitarianism, offers an informal version of the same idea. Like the classical utilitarians, his notion of equal consideration is that no one should "count" for more (or less) and, hence, that everyone's interests should be counted equally. From the bare notion of equal counting combined with a notion of the consequences to be counted, he reaches a form of utilitarianism:

> Suppose I then begin to think ethically, to the extent of simply recognizing that my own interests cannot count for more, simply because they are my own, than the interests of others. In place of my own interests, I now have to take account of the interests of all those affected by my decision. This requires me to weigh up all these interests and adopt the course of action most likely to maximize the interests of those affected. Thus I must choose the course of action which has the best consequences, on balance, for all affected. This is a form of utilitarianism.[31]

These three procedures—Rawls's original position, Ackerman's neutrality, the equal consideration route to utilitarianism—do not begin to exhaust the moral decision procedures that might plausibly purport to consider everyone's claims or interests equally or impartially. I might, equally, have considered Douglas Rae's "court of allocation,"[32] the variations of Rawls's original position that yield average utility,[33] some proposals

---

30. See n. 22 above.

31. Peter Singer, *Practical Ethics*, p. 12.

32. Douglas W. Rae, "A Principle of Simple Justice," in Peter Laslett and James Fishkin, eds., *Philosophy, Politics and Society, Fifth Series* (Oxford: Basil Blackwell; New Haven: Yale University Press, 1979).

33. J. C. Harsanyi, "Cardinal Utility in Welfare Economics and in the Theory of Risk-Taking," *Journal of Political Economy* 61 (1953).

for objectivity and impartiality developed by Thomas Nagel,[34] or my own attempts to adopt a variant of the cake cutter's analogy to problems of distributive justice.[35] All these proposals exemplify the same general strategy of argument—they purport to consider everyone's relevant claims or interests equally or impartially in the selection of first principles.[36]

There are two essential elements in any such decision procedure: (a) the account of impartiality or equal consideration; (b) the account of the interests or other relevant claims that are given equal consideration under (a). Even slight modifications in (a) or (b) can produce enormous variations in the resulting principle. The dispute between advocates of Rawlsian maximin justice and average utility, for example, finds its parallel, at the level of decision procedures, in a construction of the original position in which probabilistic calculations are ruled out (leading to Rawls's solution) and in one in which they are accepted as rational (leading to average utility). If Ackerman's argument were reformulated with utility as the material for distribution (note that his perfect technology of justice is presumed to deal successfully with problems of interpersonal comparison), it would have entirely different implications than would the same neutral dialogue applied to income, genetics, and education.[37] Or, Rawlsian social "primary goods" (liberty, equal opportunity, income, and wealth), if adopted as the notion of consequences in Singer's "equal counting" argument, would yield an aggregate maximization

34. See Thomas Nagel, *The Possibility of Altruism* (Oxford: Oxford University Press, 1979), pp. 136–42, for the ingenious proposal that each person is to be imagined splitting into several persons, living *all* their lives affected by a choice, seriatim. See also his *Limits of Objectivity*, the Tanner Lecture on Human Values, Oxford University, May 1979.

35. James S. Fishkin, *Tyranny and Legitimacy: A Critique of Political Theories* (Baltimore: Johns Hopkins University Press, 1979), chap. 12.

36. Ronald Dworkin, "Liberalism," in Stuart Hampshire, ed., *Public and Private Morality* (Cambridge: Cambridge University Press, 1978), p. 115.

37. I consider some of these alternatives applied to Ackerman's theory in my article "Can There Be a Neutral Theory of Justice?" *Ethics* 93 (January 1983): 348–56.

principle starkly different from utilitarianism in any of the senses he discusses.[38]

Any of these notions, like others waiting to be invented, would grant equal consideration, in some plausible sense, to everyone's relevant claims and interests, again in some plausible sense. *Which* senses of either (a) or (b) are most plausible is not, itself, an issue that can settled by invoking such a procedure. It is a prior issue, some solution to which must be arrived at, before the application of any such moral decision procedure is unproblematic.

Note further that we can only compare proposals differing in the details of (a) and (b) *informally*. Even if we were absolutely sure of our judgments about each procedure in turn, for any finite list of procedures, we could never know whether, after committing ourselves to a particular procedure and its resulting principle, some better procedure with different implications might not be devised.[39]

To what extent might we reasonably expect the development of such moral decision procedures to satisfy the absolutist expectations employed by our reasoners in their arguments for subjectivism? This strategy, while offering an account of moral objectivity defined by the conditions of such impartial procedures, does not purport to provide—and cannot be expected to provide—the kind of moral position that would fulfill such expectations.

Let us imagine how our subjectivist reasoners could—if they chose—maintain their positions, despite any claims that might reasonably be made on behalf of such a moral decision procedure. First, note that unlike Gewirth, proponents of these procedures grant explicitly that an "egoist" or an "amoralist"

---

38.   See Singer's notion of equal counting cited in n. 31 above. For Rawls's account of "social primary goods" see *A Theory of Justice*, pp. 62, 90−95.

39.   Rawls admits that his list of principles is informal (*A Theory of Justice*, pp. 123−26) and that for each principle we might imagine a corresponding procedure (pp. 121−22). He does not, however, draw the implications developed here from those facts. Rather, he simply treats his own proposal as "philosophically most favored" (p. 120).

who consistently refrained from making any moral claims at all could consistently avoid committing himself to such a procedure. The claim for these decision procedures is a weaker one that I will call the claim of *comparative supremacy*: those who claim validity for rival moral principles should, in some sense to be specified, come to see the appropriateness of the proposed procedure as the basis for choice.[40] However, this weaker construction of the central claim—even if it were true—would leave room for maneuver for our subjectivists that was more than sufficient for them to deny validity to the procedure. Our subjectivist reasoners do not offer rival moral principles to which they attribute validity. Since they view their own values as arbitrary tastes or preferences, they are not committed to entering the competition that these moral decision procedures purport to resolve. If the amoralist and the egoist who avoid making any substantive moral claims can avoid committing themselves to such moral decision procedures, then so can proponents of any of our other subjectivist positions. All such subjectivists refrain from making the kind of claim that would commit them to the procedure or that would enter them in the competition among rival positions that purport to be valid.

Of course, there is considerable looseness and controversy about the sense in which any of these moral decision procedures plausibly fulfills even this weakened ambition, the claim to *comparative supremacy*. I mention it only because it is the most sympathetic possible interpretation of what advocates of these procedures purport to have accomplished. And this most sympathetic possible interpretation leaves more than enough room for maneuver for our subjectivists to deny any validity or appropriateness to the procedure.

Yet this is only the beginning of the problem. Consider some list of moral decision procedures, $D_1, D_2, D_3, \ldots D_N$. Each decision procedure has its corresponding substantive principle, P_1, $P_2, P_3, \ldots P_N$, respectively. Proponents of each decision proce-

---

40. Rawls, for example, treats egoism "not as an alternative conception of right but as a challenge to any such conception" (*A Theory of Justice*, p. 136).

dure and its corresponding principle claim comparative supremacy with respect to all the alternatives in the list. How are we to judge among these competing claims to comparative supremacy? As noted before, this is not a problem that can be settled by any of the decision procedures themselves. And if one were to invent decision procedures to adjudicate among decision procedures, the same problem would arise again at one remove. Any meta-decision procedure, invented so as to support one decision procedure rather than its competitors, could be challenged by rivals supporting alternative procedures. The strategy of inventing a procedure to choose among procedures would not resolve the problem but would only raise the specter of infinite regress in chains of justificatory reasoning.

The basic difficulty is that there is no basis for adjudicating among alternative claims to comparative supremacy. Proponents of a particular principle—who would justify it by reference to a particular procedure for which they claim comparative supremacy—can always be challenged by rivals who offer precisely symmetrical claims for their own principles based on their own procedures. Proponents of a particular solution can always be challenged at the point of commitment to the proposed procedure; they can be challenged on the grounds that the construction of the procedure is *biased* in its account of impartiality or of relevant claims or interests so as to favor the proponent's principle over its rivals. The result is always open to reasonable disagreement because good-faith disputes over substantive principles can always find their parallel in good-faith disputes over moral decision procedures, that is, over the appropriate reasonable basis for resolving disputes. The issue of which procedure to adopt cannot be settled by the procedure itself. And, given the variety of procedures, each one supporting a different substantive outcome, the mere invocation of a moral decision procedure supporting one particular proposal is not enough to settle a moral disagreement.[41]

41. In this section I am elaborating an argument made more briefly in chap. 5 of my *Justice, Equal Opportunity, and the Family* (New Haven: Yale University Press, 1983).

Just as different arbitration panels can be expected to produce different results in, say, a labor-management dispute, different moral decision procedures clearly yield different principles of justice. But in a labor-management dispute the jurisdiction problem can be solved either by mutual consent of the parties involved or by recourse to the mutually acknowledged authority of a court order. But for our moral decision procedures there is no basis for actual consent, and no mutually acknowledged source of authority, tying us to one particular moral decision procedure rather than to another. There are only further moral arguments about what we ought to agree to, or about what our actual notions of morality, it is contended, would commit us to, if we thought about them as the theorist advocates.

Consider how Rawls attempts to respond to this difficulty. There is a revealing ambiguity in his account of why we should accept the particular conditions he proposes for the original position. In the last paragraph of his book he tells us that "we do in fact accept" the conditions, or that if we do not, these are conditions that we still "can be persuaded to" accept:

> Finally, we may remind ourselves that the hypothetical nature of the original position invites the question: why should we take any interest in it, moral or otherwise? Recall the answer: the conditions embodied in the description of this situation are ones that we do in fact accept. Or if we do not, then we can be persuaded to do so by philosophical considerations of the sort occasionally introduced.[42]

And if we are not or cannot actually be "persuaded," what is the basis for binding us to the results of the procedure? Rawls does not purport to answer the egoist who does not commit himself to the procedure, since we knew all along that egoism "is incompatible with what we intuitively regard as the moral point of view."[43] But if we do not accept the procedure because we would rather accept some alternative account of the moral

42. Rawls, *A Theory of Justice*, p. 587.
43. Ibid., p. 136.

point of view, some alternative decision procedure that offers what we regard as a more appealing account of impartiality or a more plausible conception of interests, then we have a jurisdictional challenge that cannot be handled so easily. At this point Rawls can only invoke the claim of "reflective equilibrium," a claim that only postpones the issue another step.

"In searching for the most favored description of this situation [the decision procedure], we work from both ends," Rawls tells us. We are to construct the choice situation and carefully examine the results, adding one weak condition to another. "By going back and forth, sometimes altering the conditions of the contractual circumstances, at others withdrawing our judgments and conforming them to principle," we eventually reach what Rawls calls "reflective equilibrium"—a state of mutual support between our considered judgments of particular cases and the decision procedure from which those judgments can be derived.[44]

Yet if each of us conscientiously goes through this process and arrives at a different "reflective equilibrium," as presumably sincere proponents of the moral decision procedures described above already have done, then reflective equilibrium becomes a framework for reasonable moral disagreement. It becomes a position with different substantive implications for different practitioners of the process. We have only to replace the pronoun "we" with the pronoun "I" and envision the resulting dissention among conscientious proponents of these differing procedures and others that might be devised.

In this sense, the charge that Ackerman directs at Rawls and other contract theorists applies as well to his own proposal:

> I take it that, in one way or another all contractarians want to convince us to approach the problem of justice as if it were (1) some hypothetical person with a particular set of preferences confronting (2) some hypothetical situation that forces us to choose one among a number of options

44. Ibid., p. 20.

open to us. . . . Now, if this characterization of the general argument is accepted, a basic problem seems plain enough. It is just too easy to manipulate the definitions of chooser and choice set to generate any conclusion that suits one's fancy.[45]

Of course, there is a sense in which Ackerman's "neutral dialogue" would not require us to imagine a "hypothetical" third party since we ourselves can engage in the dialogue. There is, furthermore, a sense in which he rejects "reflective equilibrium" since he would prescribe adherence to the implications of neutral dialogue even when our intuitions about particular cases sharply disagreed.[46] (Ackerman would legitimate euthanasia and infanticide in some cases in which he knows many of his readers will dissent.[47])

With these caveats in mind, however, the basic issue remains. The conditions applying to the choice of principles can be manipulated to support rival alternatives, each with serious advocates. While Ackerman's choice situation does not require us to imagine a hypothetical third party, it does require us to imagine ourselves under hypothetical conditions (the perfect technology of justice) in which we enter a new world from a spaceship and distribute grains of "manna."[48] As I have argued elsewhere, slight variations in the definition of neutrality in this situation, like slight variations in Rawls's original position, lead to sharply divergent outcomes.[49] The manipulability of these assumptions leaves the result open to good-faith disagreement at the point of commitment to the procedure, or at the point of claims to supremacy, for one rival procedure rather than another. Each procedure offers an account of impartiality according to which every person's claim and every rival theory is given equal consideration. But since the fundamental issue

45. Ackerman, *Social Justice in the Liberal State*, p. 337.
46. Ibid., section 65.
47. Ibid., pp. 79–80, 128–29.
48. Ibid., chaps. 1 and 2.
49. See Fishkin, "Can There Be a Neutral Theory of Justice?"

hinges on the appropriate interpretation of equal consideration, the mere fact that each theory has such an interpretation available to invoke is not enough to settle the issue. It is the beginning of the debate rather than the end of it.

This room for reasonable disagreement about the jurisdiction of rival procedures, like the room for maneuvering available to our subjectivists to deny the appropriateness of any such procedure, undermines the possibility that such a decision procedure would have to be beyond reasonable question. It would have to fulfill claims of the kind we saw made by Kant and Gewirth. And, as we saw, our subjectivists can maintain the claim that they are human actors without any requirement that they also claim "autonomy" in the Kantian sense or generic "rights" to freedom and well-being in Gewirth's sense. So long as our subjectivists maintain logical consistency in avoiding substantive moral claims that they assert or regard as valid, they can avoid moral assumptions of the kind that might provide a basis for arguing them over to the objectivist side of the controversy.

There is thus an inevitable inconclusiveness to the attempts to resolve moral disagreements by reference to a decision procedure. This inconclusiveness arises from the fact that such decision procedures are always open to jurisdictional challenge—through invocation of a rival procedure or through challenge to any such procedure. This kind of inconclusiveness means only that the results of any given procedure are not rationally unquestionable in the sense required for absolutism—precisely because the availability of rival procedures yielding divergent conclusions is, in itself, a specification of alternative senses of moral reasonableness, of alternative notions of the impartial consideration of relevant claims, that yield rational grounds for disagreeing with any particular results.

These moral decision procedures can be viewed as the most sophisticated examples of a more general strategy. Let us distinguish, broadly, between arguments for a particular moral position that are *internal*, in the sense that they depend on a characterization of morality or the moral point of view itself, and those that are *external*, in that they depend on propositions that are not part of the characterization of morality or the moral point of view, but rather, turn on other claims—for example, claims about God or the structure of the universe or human destiny. Of course, most recognizable moral positions will involve some mixture of internal and external strategies of argument at their foundation, but these elements can be separated out for analytical purposes.

The moral decision procedures just discussed represent rigorous examples of the internal strategy. It should be obvious that one might argue more informally from some characterization of the moral point of view without formalizing it in a procedure. Familiar invocations of the Golden Rule, where many crucial steps are left to common sense, have this character.[50] Clearly, everything we have said about the inconclusiveness of the rigorous and formalized versions of the strategy must also apply to looser and more informal versions. Not only are they subject to jurisdictional challenge by competing procedures, but if they are sufficiently informal they may be invoked by rival claimants, each in support of their own position. Something like this result is, of course, familiar to those who invoke the Categorical Imperative. Equally sincere proponents of competing principles may claim that they can "will" the maxims of their actions as universal laws for all mankind. The mere formal requirement that the maxim be connected to a universal law willed for all mankind can usually be invoked by rival claimants without much difficulty.[51] Hence, if we consider the

50. Alan Gewirth, "The Golden Rule Rationalized," *Midwest Studies in Philosophy* 3 (1978), offers a useful discussion of the looseness of many common inferences from the Golden Rule.

51. So long as they formulate the maxims of their actions consistently as universal laws for all mankind and so long as they claim that they can "will" the maxims in question, rival disputants cannot employ the Categorical Imperative to demonstrate the superiority of one principle over another. For further discussion see my *Limits of Obligation*, chap. 12.

Categorical Imperative, like the Golden Rule, as an informal example of a moral decision procedure, or as an informal characterization of the general form of moral reasoning, everything we have already said about the more formal versions of the argument can be applied to it.

The general point is that internal strategies of argument for a particular moral position are inevitably open to reasonable disagreement because they are open to challenge by rival positions that can also invoke a comparable internal strategy sufficiently different in its particulars as to yield competing conclusions. They are open to reasonable disagreement in the fundamental sense that rival positions can all invoke alternative conceptions of moral reasonableness (as specified by their use of the internal strategy) to support their positions.

Consider the alternative possibility of an external strategy. The credibility of an external strategy depends, of course, on the particular assumptions (external to the characterization of morality itself) invoked. Depending on the rest of a reasoner's belief system, some external strategies may appear more convincing than others. However, for our purposes, the central point is that the implications of an external strategy of justification can always be evaded with consistency by at least some construction of any of our subjectivist positions. Each of those positions has been defined so that its commitments are completely open on any questions external to the characterization of morality and the moral point of view. So while it may be the case that a particular subjectivist believes in some assumption that provides the basis for an external strategy of justification (a belief in God, for example), it is always possible for the subjectivist position in question to be formulated—and consistently defended—without any commitment to that assumption. Hence a defender of any given subjectivist position can always neutralize the relevance or jurisdictional claim of an external strategy of argument—since he can always maintain his meta-ethical position while denying whatever assumptions (external to the characterization of morality itself) provide the basis for the argument. Because it is always possible for a subjectivist to defeat an external strategy of argument in this way, such strategies cannot be expected to fulfill the absolutist expectation for principles beyond reasonable question. Although an account of moral reasonableness might be developed so that it was part of the definition of "reasonable" that a given external assumption be accepted, this approach would obviously require a controversial definition of the "morally reasonable"— controversial precisely in the sense that rival external strategies (rival religions, for example) could employ the same definitional move for *their* respective crucial external assumptions. Hence there are decisive impediments to the development of an external strategy that would provide a position beyond reasonable question.

This vulnerability to further reasonable questioning can be glimpsed in the references to "moral revelation," "God," and "religion" in the various interviews cited in chapter 3. The basic problem was aptly summarized by Sam:

> Once you fall into the trap of having to seek support from outside, once you fall into the trap of basing something on an absolute outside of yourself or outside of the world or whatever—such as God or Truth or Reason—that as soon as that absolute is brought into question, then your system of values crumbles.

Because Sam accepts expectation 1, because he requires some basis beyond reasonable question, he regards the vulnerability of any such external strategy as a "trap"—rendering his entire system vulnerable to crumbling once any such assumption is brought into question.

Any particular strategy of justification, whether external or internal, can always be neutralized in two ways. First, it can be challenged by an alternative strategy (an alternative moral decision procedure or an alternative external assumption) connected to a rival principle. Since these alternative strategies can be interpreted, in themselves, as specifying conflicting senses of moral reasonableness, they demonstrate how no position is immune from reasonable question. Second, each of our subjectivist positions can be formulated so as to evade commitment to the assumptions necessary for an external strategy. And we have already seen in detail how defenders of subjectivism can evade the jurisdiction of internal strategies. Neither strategy of justification, external or internal, can be expected to provide a credible position that would satisfy our reasoners' expectation for a position beyond reasonable question. If the absolutist expectations define appropriate conditions for moral objectivity, then the general route to subjectivism followed by our ordinary reasoners is irresistible.

Later I will question the appropriateness of such expectations. For the moment let us note how these jurisdiction problems support the conclusion reached by our ordinary reasoners that credible positions satisfying expectations 1, 4, and 5, in particular, cannot reasonably be expected. Expectation 1 requires that a position be rationally unquestionable. This expectation is undermined by the fact that any basis for such a position, whether external or internal to the characterization of morality itself, can be challenged by rival versions offering symmetrical justifications conforming to their own accounts of the morally reasonable. If particular versions of moral rationality are designed to yield particular substantive conclusions, then those interpretations of rationality can also be challenged. They are not, themselves, beyond reasonable question.

At this point the difficulties with expectation 4 should also be clear. What strategy of justification would be available if one tried to be a "strictly unbiased observer," that is, one who was "completely neutral between alternative possible moral perspectives and initial assumptions"? Such an observer could not employ any particular external strategy, for that would require reliance on the initial assumptions of one rival moral advocate as opposed to that of another. Alternatively, such a neutral observer could not rely on any particular characterization of morality or of the moral point of view, as opposed to that advocated in support of rival positions. Such a move would also require reliance on the moral perspective or initial assumptions of one moral advocate as opposed to that of another. In other words, there is every reason to believe that the kind of neutral perspective required for the "strictly unbiased observer" of our fourth argument would offer no basis for argument at all. It is a kind of *reductio ad absurdum* in the quest to avoid bias: it completely eliminates bias toward any particular position only by eliminating, in the end, any basis for any particular position.

Turning to expectation 5, the possibilities for reasonable moral disagreement revealed by the jurisdiction problem illustrate the decisive impediments to fulfillment of this expectation. The mere requirement of conscientiousness—that persons be motivated only to determine what is morally right—does little, if anything, to limit the strategies of justification that the proponents of a moral position may invoke. Proponents of conflicting principles may with equal sincerity and rigor buttress their positions by refering to the Golden Rule, Kant's Categorical Imperative, Rawls's original position, Ackerman's neutral dialogue, and many others. As we have already seen, these strategies yield enormously divergent results. Equally conscientious and, indeed, equally rigorous positions clearly can be starkly incompatible. Expectation 5, that an objectively valid moral position be compatible with all such conscientious conclusions, becomes untenable once the possibilities for sincere moral disagreement are realized. Once more, we can endorse the route by which our reasoners concluded that they could not reasonably expect to fulfill this expectation. However, they concluded that nonfulfillment of this expectation made subjectivism inescapable. Alternately, they might have rejected the expectation itself—a strategy we shall follow in section 4.5 below.

4.3. The Foreseeability Problem

Recall the second and third arguments for subjectivism we encountered earlier. In the second argument Doug contended that the "complexity" of moral experience would overwhelm principles constructed as "rigid laws." Jonathan assumed that valid principles must be "absolute" and hence must be "inviolable." Because the process of envisioning credible exceptions seems to be forever open to continuation, he abandons the quest for inviolable principles (other than self-interest, which he does not regard as a moral principle but would hold to, inviolably, nevertheless). Nick adds the argument that the inevitable multiplicity of values makes conflict among them unavoidable—making an "ideal" or "absolute" system impossible.

The third argument was closely related. It focused on the inevitability not of exceptions but of indeterminacies and cases that were undecidable within the confines of a given position. Because our reasoners assumed that a "valid" or "objective" position must prescribe solutions to any moral question, they regarded such indeterminacies as a fatal defect, undermining any claims to validity for such a position.

In both arguments a crucial factor is the inherent *unforeseeability* of the full range of difficult cases to which any position will apply.[52] The complexity of moral experience produces new issues, dilemmas, and conflicts with other values that make exceptions and indeterminacies inevitable for any given position as already constructed. Let us pursue this line of argument further. Imagine a panel of *perfect* moral judges capable of judging *any* particular cases presented before them. We might imagine a panel of judges operating with complete consensus; or we might imagine ourselves, endowed with such powers, as members of the panel. In any case, let us assume for purposes of argument that there are never any reasonable grounds for disputing the resolutions of particular cases dictated by these perfect moral judges.

Of course, this is a heroically optimistic and counterfactual assumption. It is meant to dramatize, however, the fact that even such an idealized panel of perfect judges could not provide

52. In this section I elaborate an argument I made more briefly in chap. 5 of my *Justice, Equal Opportunity, and the Family.*

us with a moral position that would avoid the foreseeability problem. No substantive moral position based on inferences from a finite sequence of particular cases could credibly presume to satisfy expectations 2 and 3—the expectations that the resulting positions, as defined, hold without exception and resolve any case that might possibly present itself. Our inference from any finite sequence of already completed cases to a general moral position is an inductive one. It carries with it implications for an open-ended class of possible cases in addition to the sequence from which it has been inferred. Even if all the cases thus far decided were resolved by perfect moral judges endowed with superhuman powers, such powers would not produce for us a general moral position we could credibly offer as fulfilling these two expectations.

The difficulty is that such a general moral position, even if it were based on a sequence of perfect resolutions of particular cases, would have to consist in more than the event-specific descriptions of those cases already resolved. If it were to be a general moral position, applying to an open-ended class of possible cases, it would have to specify certain descriptive dimensions employed for singling out the preferred states of affairs or courses of conduct prescribed for future cases as they presented themselves. However, these descriptive dimensions employed for singling out the prescribed choices will, inevitably, amount to *incomplete descriptions* of the preferred alternatives—incomplete descriptions of the states of affairs or courses of conduct prescribed.

This necessary incompleteness opens the resulting general position to a crucial source of vulnerability. It is always possible that *other* aspects of the partially described states of affairs or courses of conduct will be of sufficient importance—to any credible moral position—that they will require a different resolution. The element of moral complexity that clinches the difficulty is that these moral issues of possibly overriding importance are inherently unforeseeable. If we could, in some way, enumerate them, or know that we had anticipated *all* of them, then we might build into our general moral positions provisions for the solution of those difficult cases. But there is no basis for our presuming that we have ever completely anticipated such cases. Barring some unforeseen breakthrough in moral methodology, our positions must be constructed without the benefit of any such complete enumeration or anticipation of possibly overriding factors. Without such an enumeration, we can expect any general moral position—even one constructed from the decisions of perfect moral judges in particular cases—to yield exceptions and indeterminacies in new cases as they arise. Unanticipated factors of moral relevance can be expected to crop up as new cases present themselves (a) so as to require exceptions to the prescriptions required by any general moral position, as already constructed, and (b) so as to support new prescriptions for issues about which the moral position, as already constructed, says nothing. Revisions of type a violate the expectation that the position will not require exceptions; revisions of type b violate the expectation that the position will be sufficient to determine answers to any moral question. As new factors present themselves with new cases, the proponent of any given general moral position must make the revisions required for particular cases or relinquish the claim to credibility for the position, as already constructed.

The difficulty is reminiscent of the story of the monkey's paw. An English couple acquire a magic talisman, a monkey's paw, that will grant them three wishes. Their wish for money, two hundred pounds, is answered by a messenger offering it to them in condolence for their son's death in an accident at work. Their second wish, to have their son back, is answered by the appearance of an agonized apparition. They then got their third wish, that this apparition go away.[53]

The couple's three wishes, like the prescriptions in any general moral position, pick out certain dimensions of the desired alternatives, dimensions that must incompletely describe

53. Laurence H. Tribe, "Policy Science: Analysis or Ideology?" *Philosophy and Public Affairs* 2, no. 1 (Fall 1972): 102–03.

the states of affairs or courses of conduct that are prescribed. Just as the couple had each of its wishes fulfilled but with accompanying factors so terrible that they could only regret their fulfillment, so may any general moral position be adhered to, but with accompanying factors so terrible that its proponents would view its fulfillment with extreme regret in particular cases.

Consider the vulnerability of some typical political principles commonly invoked in serious debate. There are conditions under which utilitarianism will justify slavery;[54] there are conditions under which Rawls's theory will violate both equality and utilitarianism so as to distribute less in total, less equally;[55] there are conditions under which equality will make everyone, including those at the bottom, worse off;[56] there are conditions under which any procedural principle of democracy will legitimate tyrannous outcomes inflicted on some portion of the population.[57] In each case we might reformulate our initial version of the principle so as to include provisions for the particular objectionable cases. But this process is continually open to repetition; the flood of counterexamples, many of them unexpected, directed at Rawls,[58] Nozick,[59] and utilitarianism[60] in recent debates, exemplifies how the process of finding counterexamples fully compatible with any extant position, as defined, may continue.

In another work I have explored counterexamples that can be arrayed against most of the principles currently prominent

54. Rawls, *A Theory of Justice*, pp. 158–59.

55. Rae, "A Principle of Simple Justice." This criticism applies to Rawls's general conception and to the difference principle (that the minimum share of income and wealth be maximized).

56. Rawls, *A Theory of Justice*, p. 144.

57. See Fishkin, *Tyranny and Legitimacy*, chap. 8.

58. For a representative collection see Norman Daniels, ed., *Reading Rawls: Critical Studies of A Theory of Justice* (New York: Basic Books, 1975).

59. For a representative collection see Jeffrey Paul, ed., *Reading Nozick: Essays on Anarchy, State and Utopia* (Totowa, New Jersey: Rowman and Littlefield, 1981). See also Fishkin, *Tyranny and Legitimacy*, chap. 9.

60. For a good summary of the emerging anti-utilitarian consensus in recent liberal political theory, see Hart, "Between Utility and Rights."

in contemporary political theory—procedural principles such as majority rule and unanimity, structural principles such as equality, maximin justice, and utilitarianism, and absolute rights principles such as Nozick's side constraint theory. These counterexamples reflect the hand of the monkey's paw in the parable just cited. Each is compatible with complete fulfillment of the states of affairs or courses of conduct specified by the principles under discussion. Yet in each case *other* elements of the incompletely described situation or policy are so terrible that reasonable proponents of these positions would surely wish the prescribed result to be avoided in those cases.[61] We could be reasonably confident that our position was invulnerable to such further attacks only if we had some strategy for completely specifying, in advance, the full range of crucial factors that might present themselves—the full range of overriding claims, of new moral issues, and of possible dilemmas that might require the principle, as constructed, to be reformulated. Lacking the kind of methodological breakthrough that would be required even for our perfect moral judges to conclude that their general moral positions credibly satisfied expectations 2 and 3 (holding without exception and determining answers to any moral question), we must conclude that it is unreasonable to expect that we will arrive at a position satisfying such expectations. None of us, I presume, can plausibly claim to be a perfect moral judge. If we substituted ourselves for the perfect moral judges in resolving some finite sequence of particular cases, we would find some particularly difficult cases both controversial and debatable. Hence there is all the more reason to doubt that we can arrive at a general moral position that will be adequate to the complexity of all the new issues that may present themselves.

61. I have made this more general argument in *Tyranny and Legitimacy*, part 2.

One target of this argument is what might be called the *inductive* strategy of moral justification.[62] The internal and external strategies discussed in the last section are typically employed in an essentially *deductive* manner. We are asked to assume the applicability of a moral decision procedure (or some other, more informal, account of the moral point of view) and then to accept the implications that follow from it (or that are at least compatible with it, as in Ackerman's case).[63] In any case, the decision procedure is placed at the foundation and other principles are derived from it. Of course, if we follow Rawls's method of "reflective equilibrium," as noted earlier, we attempt to combine this deductive strategy with an inductive one. Our considered judgment of particular cases provides an independent basis, one which, Rawls hopes, can be employed so as to work back to the decision procedure and to the general principles derivable from it. Nevertheless, the portion of Rawls's method that would have us work from the decision procedure to the resulting principles is essentially deductive. Similarly, the external strategy is essentially deductive in that certain religious or metaphysical beliefs are placed at the foundation of a system from which moral principles are derived. Clearly, in raising the infinite regress problems discussed in the first argument, our moral reasoners presumed that a justification for their moral position, were it possible, would take this form.

But there is also the possibility of a strategy that is essentially inductive in its generalization from particular cases. This alternative can be considered the other half of Rawls's method of reflective equilibrium. Furthermore, it is the most obvious

62. The inductive strategy can be considered a subcategory of internal strategies because both the particular judgments and the general principles inferred from them are internal to the characterization of morality.

63. Ackerman's general strategy is deductive. His principles are derived from the neutrality, rationality, and consistency constraints and from whatever other assumptions can be introduced into the argument without violating those constraints.

target for our thought experiment involving a sequence of decisions by perfect moral judges. However, the foreseeability problem is not restricted in its range of application to this inductive strategy. So long as our considered judgments of particular cases as they arise affect the determination of what is a credible moral position, the difficulties just sketched have to be faced, even if our strategy of justification is essentially deductive. If we assume the applicability of a given decision procedure and find its implications provisionally acceptable for the cases we can think of, we still have to face the unforeseeable range of future cases that may require exceptions or reformulations. So long as we lack a method of enumerating or anticipating the new moral issues that will arise with particular cases, we have no basis for concluding that our position, as formulated, will hold proof against further exceptions and reformulations.

Now, we might imagine a strategy of argument that steadfastly refused to endow our considered judgments of particular cases with any independent standing or credibility. Ackerman, in admitting that his readers may be troubled by some particular implications of his procedure (for example, implications permitting infanticide and destruction of the Grand Canyon under certain conditions),[64] would have us hold to the procedure and its resulting principles, come what may. But if we find the particular implications of a moral decision procedure sufficiently troubling, surely this should lead us, quite reasonably, to bring the procedure itself into question—comparing it with rival procedures that also purport to consider everyone's claims impartially or equally. Given the variety of procedures, and the contested and controversial jurisdictional claims at issue among them, the basis for any given procedure is not so strong that we must cling to it regardless of *any* of its implications for particular cases.[65]

---

64. See Ackerman, *Social Justice in the Liberal State*, pp. 128–29.

65. The conflict among rival principles and their corresponding procedures is "essentially contested" in Gallie's sense. It is like the competition for a championship in which each team has its own rules for determining the winner.

Once we are willing to endow our considered judgments of particular cases with independent standing or credibility, then strategies of justification for particular substantive positions must face the problem that the inherent unforeseeability of crucial moral factors stands as an impediment to satisfaction of expectations 2 and 3 (the expectations that a position hold without exception and that it resolve any moral problem). This impediment applies whether our strategy of justification for a particular position, as formulated, is essentially inductive or deductive in the manner described earlier. All this supports the conclusion that we cannot reasonably expect to arrive at positions that will never require exceptions or reformulations for new cases. As noted earlier, this does not mean that we must follow our ordinary reasoners to their conclusion that morality must be "subjective" or "arbitrary." If we reject the crucial premises of the argument—expectations 2 and 3—we can accept the possibility of exceptions and indeterminacies and, nevertheless, avoid the conclusion that the resulting position lacks validity. I will pursue this strategy in section 4.5. In the meantime, one remaining expectation must still be discussed.

4.4. The Overload Problem

The sixth argument presumed that an objective moral position would have to apply with strict impartiality, that is, with no special regard for an agent's own interests, situation, or relations with others. Our ordinary reasoners were troubled by the implications of such a moral assumption when applied consistently to the world's problems. They hesitated to commit themselves to obligations in the Heinz case, for example, because they were aware of the multitude of compelling claims that could be made on behalf of the starving and dispossessed in many far-off countries. Viewing all these claims with strict

---

See W. B. Gallie, *Philosophy and the Historical Understanding* (London: Chatto and Windus, 1964), chap. 8. See also John N. Gray, "On the Contestability of Social and Political Concepts," *Political Theory* 5, no. 3 (August 1977).

impartiality would produce demands more overwhelming than they could either believe or accept.

Brian traces out this basic line of argument in raising the question of what he should do about the "poor and hungry starving in India":

> Whatever argument I use to give to one, I have to [use to] give to another. And so I completely wipe out my own resources doing that. So I arbitrarily decide which ones I give to and which ones I don't. It doesn't seem to me that I have any real moral obligation—in principle—to help one. Because for me to fulfill that moral obligation, I wipe myself out. Because to help one means to help all. To help all means to wipe myself out.

Given that the same argument can be used on behalf of any starving person, Brian cannot "arbitrarily" select only a few. If he admits the requirement to act as a matter of obligation in one case, he has to admit it for all the equivalent cases, and this would open the door to demands so enormous that he would be "wiped out." David offers a similar argument which he responds to with his "gravity theory," according to which he values most those closest to him. But although this strategy avoids the overwhelming demands of a strictly impartial position, its bias toward those who are close to him prevents it from being "objective." The necessity he sees for the "gravity" strategy is one of the reasons he offers for giving up on "such a thing as objective right," about which he concludes that there is "no such thing."

Jonathan makes the argument even clearer by breaking it down into incremental contributions to CARE. He asks about each one whether it "is going to be more important to you than to that person starving in India." If one went so far in one's sacrifices as Gandhi did, and gave up virtually all one's possessions, then one would have arrived at a position that Jonathan would "respect." But "Joe Blow who lives in a house and has a washing machine and gives money to CARE" is simply being "hypocritical" and has not arrived at a defensible position, according to Jonathan. Real altruism of the sort necessary for a consistent and defensible moral position would require that he give away "everything, until he gave so much away that he was as poor as the poorest person—which he obviously wouldn't do."

These reasoners are troubled by a fundamental problem. If they consider the state of the world with strict impartiality, then according to any plausible assessment of relevant claims or interests they are easily led to moral demands that are overwhelming beyond the point they can find credible or acceptable. Their solution is to abandon the effort to determine moral requirements with strict impartiality. Since they consider strict impartiality a necessary condition for a position to be defensible or valid, they must then conclude that their own positions are merely "subjective" or "arbitrary."

At least three crucial questions may be asked about this argument. First, is it true that strict impartiality, when combined with any plausible assessment of relevant claims or interests, must lead to overwhelming moral demands? Second, should we conclude that "overwhelming moral demands" (in some sense to be specified) are not credible or acceptable? Third, if we answer yes to the first two questions, is there any way out of the problem but to deny objective validity? A positive answer to the last question will concern us in section 4.5. For the moment, let us consider the first two questions.

If all moral claims are judged by a given moral agent with strict impartiality, it is clear that there are conditions under which the results become overwhelming. Our reasoners have in mind the plight of the millions of starving people, many of them refugees, in the Third and Fourth worlds in areas ranging at various times from India and Bangladesh to parts of Africa, particularly the Sahel. They suppose, not unreasonably, that at certain levels of collective effort, additional small contributions to reputable organizations will facilitate the delivery of surplus foodstuffs to starving refugees and, therefore, that those contributions have a likelihood of saving lives (or at least of preventing very great harm such as malnutrition). I will not dispute these empirical assumptions; they apply more clearly to some cases than to others.

Given this characterization of the problem, if I attempt to determine my obligations with strict impartiality, any plausible assessment of claims or interests easily yields enormous requirements for action.

It is difficult to avoid the assumption that imminent starvation defines a relevant moral claim of a critically important kind and that the interest anyone would have in avoiding imminent starvation would be of paramount importance. When this interest of the refugee in avoiding imminent starvation is compared with the interests at stake for one of our reasoners in making a small contribution, the comparison—required by any strictly impartial consideration of the problem—produces virtually irresistible pressure in favor of a further contribution. If he is strictly impartial, our reasoner must view himself—along with all the starving refugees—as just one person among others. The marginal effect on his situation of a five- or ten-dollar contribution is minor. The marginal effect on the refugee's situation is dramatic by comparison.

A variety of moral decision procedures embodying strict impartiality easily lead to this conclusion. If I apply the Golden Rule to the problem of starving refugees, then I must put myself in the place of those affected by my action (or inaction) in the decision to contribute. If I apply Rawls's original position to the problem, then I must design a principle while taking seriously the possibility that I will turn out to be the worst-off person. If I apply the calculations of a utilitarian spectator, the marginal utility to the starving person of being saved dramatically outweighs the marginal loss to me from a small contribution (and if I have altruistic preferences I may not be significantly worse off at all).

Each of these moral decision procedures easily supports the conclusion that I must contribute.[66] The difficulty that troubled our reasoners, however, was more dramatic, namely, that once the same argument is admitted in one case, it can be applied equally to a host of successive cases. Jonathan even considered it incrementally, arguing from the effects of the 200th dollar, the 201st dollar, etc. The disparity in effects at the margin (on him and on the starving refugee) was so little altered by each increased contribution that he quickly found himself on a slippery slope where, in order to maintain a defensible position, he would have to become "as poor as the poorest person."

However, the slippery slope need not carry us as far as Jonathan envisages in order for it to take on radically disturbing implications. At least two familiar limits on moral demands inevitably become overloaded by consistent application of this argument to a large enough number of cases. These limits can be specified as:

1. *The Cutoff for Heroism:* Certain levels of sacrifice cannot be morally required of any given individual.
2. *The Robustness of the Zone of Indifference:* A substantial proportion of any individual's actions fall appropriately within the zone of indifference or permissibly free personal choice.[67]

The first limit is merely the notion that sufficient sacrifice (including sufficiently great risk of sacrifice) renders beyond the call of duty an act that might otherwise be obligatory. It is more than can reasonably be demanded or required; performing such an action is unusually noble or heroic, but failing to perform it is not morally blameworthy. In that sense it becomes discretion-

66. See Fishkin, *The Limits of Obligation*, especially section 19, for an application of these moral decision procedures to the famine relief problem.
67. I discuss these two limits in greater detail in *The Limits of Obligation*, sections 3, 4, and 7.

ary in a way that distinguishes it from the moral requirements defined by duties and obligations.

Morally speaking, our actions can be classified into three broad classifications: (a) the zone of *moral requirement*, defined by duties or obligations: it is right or morally praiseworthy if we conform to these requirements and wrong or morally blame-worthy if we fail to; (b) the zone of *supererogation*, defined by actions beyond the call of duty and any other discretionary actions that it would be praiseworthy for us to perform but not blameworthy were we to fail to perform them; (c) the zone of *indifference*, defined by actions that fall under no morally pre-scriptive classifications of right or wrong, good or bad: it is neither praiseworthy if we perform them nor blameworthy if we fail to perform them. The zone of moral indifference defines an area of permissibly free personal choice where we can, morally speaking, do as we please. The second limit specified above is merely the claim that it is appropriate for a substantial propor-tion of our actions to fall into this classification.

It is an unspoken assumption of the way most of us live that morality is reserved for special occasions. Many, if not most, of the actions we normally perform over the course of a day are not performed out of duty or obligation and are not heroic. Raising no moral issues one way or the other, they are morally indif-ferent.

Perhaps it is not defensible that we should live this way. Some traditional ways of life and modern religious sects regard every minute aspect of life as determined by moral dictates of one sort or another. But the way of life we commonly take for granted in modern secular Western moral culture is clearly quite different and does not conform to this assumption. We might regard this second limit, the robust zone of indifference, as a corollary of the first, the cutoff for heroism. For any of us to give up virtually *all* the normal activities whose appropriate-ness we take for granted and replace them with actions deter-mined by duties or obligations would constitute a substantial sacrifice, a sacrifice of the sort that might be characterized as beyond the call of duty. It would constitute a substantial sacrifice precisely because it would require us to give up an entire way of life. If we were to give up our present activities and replace them entirely with actions prescribed by duty or obligation, we would be making substantial sacrifices, since our present projects, our plans of life, would have to be relinquished or abandoned. Hence the assumption of a robust zone of indifference can be rationalized as a particular demarcation of the cutoff for heroism (but not, of course, the only one, that is, not the only relevant kind of sacrifice rendering acts beyond the call of duty).[68]

I believe that our ordinary reasoners have assumed the appropriateness of something like these two limits on moral demands—the cutoff for heroism and the robust zone of indifference. In attempting to refine and elaborate their argument, I will employ these two assumptions as explanations of the sense in which moral demands will, at some point, require too much—too much in the sacrifice of one's interests or too much in the sacrifice of one's time, effort, or freedom to live according to one's own life plan.

When an individual moral agent employs strict impartiality in considering his obligations to contribute to famine relief or to other collective actions intended to eliminate great suffering, any plausible consideration of claims or interests quickly yields conclusions that overwhelm the two limits just defined.

When the state of the world is such that a strictly impartial consideration of all relevant claims or interests yields a requirement that a given agent act, let us call that an *obligation-determining situation*. Given the empirical assumptions mentioned above about famine relief, each small contribution will lower only incrementally and imperceptibly the number of obligation-determining situations facing each of us. Under the conditions of imperfect moral cooperation that commonly

---

68. So long as money, time, and effort are *among* the relevant interests whose sacrifice can trigger the cutoff, the argument goes through.

apply, and given the state of the world at present, there are enormous numbers of human beings who are available to make moral claims on us of the most basic sort. If I were to give, say, half my income to famine relief, it would still be the case that on my (junior faculty) salary another small contribution of five or ten dollars would, even at that cumulative level of sacrifice, be small in its comparative effects on me—as those effects might be compared, with strict impartiality, to the benefits to those helped. Hence, by a strictly impartial consideration of interests, I could reasonably be faced with further requirements to contribute and further requirements to act. These requirements would follow from the condition of the countless refugees waiting to be helped by someone. Yet, I believe, if I were to go so far as to give half my income, I would already have triggered the cutoff for heroism by any plausible construction. Yet strict impartiality easily requires that I continue giving after that point. By a strictly impartial consideration of claims, the fact that I have already acted does not insulate me from further moral demands. And in a world of imperfect moral cooperation, where others fail to do their full share, I should continue to conclude that more persons will be helped if I act than if I do not. I can assume, in other words, that the response will not outstrip the appeals and that we will not run out of poor and starving people who might be helped. They will remain in sufficient numbers to overwhelm the cutoff for heroism and the robust sphere of indifference asserted by any of us considering the problem as isolated individuals, as separate moral actors.

The famine relief problem brings home a more general difficulty. If any given agent is faced with a large enough number of obligation-determining situations, the interests at stake for the agent, however small for each required act, may accumulate so as to overwhelm any reasonable construction of the cutoff for heroism and of the robust sphere of indifference. The resources, time, effort, and interests sacrificed will at some point add up to more than could reasonably have been demanded as a matter of obligation. Let us call this the *overload* problem. The central point, for our purposes, is that a strictly impartial consideration of interests disconnects an agent's present obligation from his own past history of action. Provided that one is capable of further sacrifice, one is eligible for further moral demands, just like any other person. Given the number of obligation-determining situations produced by the number of worthy recipients throughout the world, each of us, when we consider the problem with strict impartiality as isolated individuals, arrives at obligations that can, quite reasonably, be interpreted as overloading the two limits we have assumed.[69]

The argument just outlined requires only the following components: (a) strict impartiality in the consideration of individual obligation; (b) assumptions about individual claims or interests that give priority to the claims of starving refugees over those at stake for (comparatively) affluent Westerners in the consideration of marginal contributions; (c) the empirical assumptions about famine relief specifying that further contributions will have the desired effects; (d) the two limits on appropriate moral demands, the cutoff for heroism and the robust zone of indifference.

Our reasoners have reached the conclusion that (a), (b), and (c) together produce requirements that overload (d). My discussion here is meant to support them in this analysis. Their reaction to this conundrum is, basically, to maintain (d) but sacrifice (a). In the next section I will follow them in this basic strategy as well. However, their further inference from the sacrifice of (a) is that, because strict impartiality is a necessary condition for objective validity, the resulting moral positions must be subjective or arbitrary. At this point I will suggest that we need not conclude so much from the argument. We can sacrifice (a) and still avoid subjectivism as a conclusion.

These are not, of course, the only possibilities. We might attempt to undermine (c), the relevant empirical assumptions.

69. A more extended treatment of this overload problem can be found in my *Limits of Obligation*, sections 7, 8, 9, 18, 19. The version presented there is more complex in that I argue from strict impartiality to general obligations (as contrasted to special ones) and from general obligations, in turn, to overload.

Such a strategy would require cynicism of an extreme kind about the efficacy and integrity of all famine relief efforts. More important for our purposes, such a strategy would not respond to the theoretical problem—that our basic assumptions combine in an untenable fashion for relevant possible cases, cases that may certainly arise even if they do not, in fact, apply at one particular time or another. Undermining (c) would not, in other words, really respond to the theoretical problem.

Alternatively, we might undermine or deny (b), the assumptions about individual claims or interests that give priority to the claims of starving refugees over those at stake at the margin for our potential contributors. However, the contrast in the interests at stake between starving refugees and comparatively affluent citizens of the Western developed countries is so stark that I will not pursue this response here.

The remaining line of response would be to undermine or deny (d), the two limits we have assumed on moral demands. These two limits were regarded as conditions necessary for credible moral positions. Moral requirements so demanding as to overwhelm limits of this kind were regarded by our reasoners as implausible. These limits are not only common constituents of the way we think about morality, they are also common constituents of the way most of us live. However, we can imagine logically consistent positions and ways of life according to which they would be sacrificed (Jonathan mentions Gandhi as an example).

For our purposes I need only note that this last strategy, sacrificing the limits, can be developed in a defensible and consistent manner. It would, however, open us to the conclusion that we are now required, as a matter of duty or obligation, to undertake moral sacrifices of the kind we had previously reserved for heroes or saints. Although this may, in fact, be the appropriate resolution to the problem, I will outline in the next section an alternative, less radical strategy—one that does not require such a vast transformation in the moral assumptions and ways of life most of us have adopted.

4.5. Avoiding Subjectivism

Our ordinary reasoners arrived at subjectivism through recurrent use of the following general pattern of argument:

1. An objectively valid moral position must have characteristic X (specified by one of the six expectations).
2. Any credible moral position I can reasonably expect to arrive at lacks characteristic X.
3. Therefore, any credible moral position I can reasonably expect to arrive at cannot be objectively valid (and, hence, must be "subjective" or "arbitrary").

In the last three sections I have attempted to develop further the arguments supporting step 2. Everything said thus far is meant to buttress the conclusion of our ordinary reasoners that we cannot reasonably expect to arrive at positions satisfying the six expectations. The crucial point, however, is that the inference to subjectivism, the conclusion in step 3, does not necessarily follow, provided we can challenge premise 1 of the argument—provided we can challenge the claims of the six expectations to define necessary conditions for objective validity.

If the scheme of ethical positions introduced in chapter 2 above and pictured in chart 2 is correct, then we could accept all the arguments offered here against fulfillment of the six expectations, and the inference to subjectivism would still be avoidable. The central point is that position III—minimal objectivism in the scheme—does not require fulfillment of *any* of the six expectations. Its principles do not lay claim to being rationally unquestionable; they do not necessarily hold without exception; they do not presume to resolve every moral question; they do not lay claim to the neutral perspective of an external observer; they do not have to agree with every conscientious moral decision; and, finally, they do not have to determine individual obligations with strict impartiality. If position III is merely admitted as a *possible* alternative, then the route to subjectivism is no longer inescapable.

However, proponents of subjectivism can consistently maintain their positions by simply refusing to admit this possibility. Indeed, if they approach the problem with the absolutist expectations uncovered here, position III will fall so far short of those expectations that it will provide a disturbingly insecure—and perhaps quite unconvincing—foundation for moral judgment.

The debate between our subjectivist reasoners and any defender of objectivity in ethics must turn on the possibility of a middle ground between positions fulfilling the absolutist expectations, on the one hand, and the various subjectivist positions, on the other. This middle ground is defined in our scheme by both position III and, for all the expectations except the one requiring no exceptions, position II, rigorism.

We have already discussed an extensively developed family of theories that occupy this middle ground. Recent liberal theories of social justice—based on impartiality or the equal consideration of relevant claims or interests—fill this role. Indeed, the thrust of my argument in the jurisdiction and foreseeability problems is that it is more plausible to relegate those theories to position III (where they fulfill the role required by our argument perfectly) than to position II (where the fit is imperfect because they would then claim to hold without exception).

The jurisdiction problem makes evident how these procedures cannot presume (and, for the most part, do not presume) any basis that is beyond reasonable question. Any such claim would be open to challenge in two ways. First, there are alternative moral decision procedures that challenge the jurisdiction of any particular procedure to decide moral questions with unique priority. Rival procedures (and rival impartial perspectives construed more informally) can make symmetrical claims for their respective notions of impartiality and for their respective notions of relevant claims or interests. These symmetrical claims constitute rival accounts of moral reasonableness. Hence no one interpretation can credibly presume, in the face of such rivals, that it is beyond all reasonable question. As a result, any claim to unique priority for such a procedure will inevitably be controversial since it is open to reasonable disagreement. Second, the room for maneuver that we saw such decision procedures grant to the amoralist or egoist provides another sense in which they are not beyond reasonable question. Their jurisdiction can be consistently denied by those who are willing to refrain entirely from making rival moral claims they regard as valid. If such a subjectivist or amoralist were then to restrict his account of rationality or reasonableness to logical consistency, then the fact that he could consistently deny such a moral decision procedure would in itself reveal a sense in which the procedure was not beyond reasonable question.

It is worth noting, however, that this family of moral decision procedures—the liberal theories of justice founded on impartiality, or equal concern and respect for relevant claims or interests—generally presume to satisfy the expectation of no exceptions, at least within some limited domain. In other words, they generally aspire to offer us versions of position II rather than position III. Rawls aspires to solve the "priority problem" and thus to arrive at principles that hold without exception, without "intuitionistic" balancing against any competing considerations, once the "veil of ignorance" is lifted.[70] The impartial spectator of the utilitarians provides a principle that, problems of measurement and implementation aside, never has to be balanced against competing moral considerations, at least in theory. Ackerman's neutral dialogue similarly leads to a unique solution, although he admits that the possibility that it may be employed in justification of rival principles cannot be ruled out.[71]

However, with the exception of the utilitarian spectator, these procedures make such claims only within a carefully limited sphere. For example, Rawls's principles of justice are pro-

70. Rawls, *A Theory of Justice*, pp. 41–45, 63.
71. Ackerman, *Social Justice in the Liberal State*, pp. 12–15.

posed only for the problem of justice for a given society under conditions of "ideal theory." They are not proposed for international distributive justice, for problems of "partial compliance" or extreme scarcity within the boundaries of a given society.[72] Furthermore, they are not proposed for problems of individual moral choice. While the possibility is left open for developments in this general method for individual choice, the adaptation enmeshes the theory in a host of new issues.[73] Hence, even if Rawls's own most ambitious claims for his principles of justice were accepted, this would leave open the possibility that a Rawlsian position, once committed to areas outside his carefully restricted problem (social justice under ideal conditions within a given society), would fit within position III rather than position II—because at least some of its principles would leave room for exceptions and for an intuitionistic balancing of competing considerations.[74]

It is worth noting that Ronald Dworkin's account of constitutional jurisprudence fits precisely this pattern. He identifies his root notion of "equal concern and respect" with Rawls's original position but at the same time defines a plurality of "principles" with varying "weights" that are, to varying degrees, to be balanced against competing considerations of "policy."[75] The result is a systematic variant of what Rawls calls "intuitionism" but one that has its foundation in an account of equal concern and respect identified with the original position.

Elsewhere I have argued in detail how Ackerman's framework may be employed in support of a variety of competing

72. Rawls, *A Theory of Justice*, pp. 7–17, 242–48. Charles R. Beitz has attempted to extend the Rawlsian argument to international relations. See his *Political Philosophy and International Relations* (Princeton: Princeton University Press, 1979).

73. An example of such an extension can be found in David A. J. Richards, *A Theory of Reasons for Action* (Oxford: Oxford University Press, 1971).

74. For some similar speculations, see Joel Feinberg "Rawls and Intuitionism," in Norman Daniels, ed., *Reading Rawls*.

75. Dworkin, *Taking Rights Seriously*, pp. 22–28, 90–100.

conclusions.[76] But rather than tie the issue to the particular characteristics of any given theory, I need make only a general point here. The foreseeability problem provides general grounds for questioning whether any particular extant principle (or any set of principles in lexical order) linked to some particular decision procedure as now constructed should be interpreted as holding in all spheres of choice without exception—no matter what future cases present themselves. Even if we believed that one of these proposals had completely resolved the restricted problem of social justice (distribution within a given society under ideal conditions), this would leave so much room for exceptions and qualifications in other spheres of social and individual choice that there would still be good grounds for limiting our aspirations to position III. Furthermore, how confident can we be of any particular resolution, even to the restricted problem of social justice, when we have no way of testing our considered judgments against the full range of possibly overriding factors that may present themselves? If we commit ourselves to apply a principle without exceptions or further qualifications, then we are foreclosing our room for maneuver in future difficult cases that are, at present, unforeseeable. There is no doubt that these new theories of social justice fulfill, at least, the requirements for position III. Their aspiration, within restricted spheres, to fulfill the requirements for position II has mired them in controversy. Rather than distract our meta-ethical argument here with substantive controversies attaching to particular theories, I need only point to the family of theories together as illustrating the middle ground between absolutism and subjectivism.

Any of the liberal theories of justice discussed earlier can be viewed as illustrative of position III rather than position II, provided that certain complexities are admitted. The foreseeability problem may prompt us to regard the proposed prin-

76. Fishkin, "Can There Be a Neutral Theory of Justice?"

ciples as overrideable in future difficult cases. Or the many criticisms and counterexamples already directed at each proposal in the published literature may prompt us to permit exceptions for competing moral considerations.[77] Or we can easily imagine rigorous principles proposed for one sphere supplemented by a variety of competing "intuitionistic" considerations applied to other spheres (such as personal choice), yielding a general position that conforms to position III rather than position II.

These theories fail to conform to expectation 1 because they are not rationally unquestionable. When supplemented by the complexities just discussed, they can plausibly be interpreted as failing to conform to expectation 2. What about expectation 3? There is no reason to suppose that a liberal theory of justice, founded on impartiality, should presume to resolve every moral question. As already noted, these theories typically aspire to resolve moral issues only within a restricted sphere—the problem of distributive justice within a given society under ideal conditions. If we regard any one of these theories as successful for its chosen problem, why should we undermine its validity because of its failure to resolve *other* problems, problems outside its proposed area of application? With the notable exception of utilitarianism,[78] any of these liberal theories will respond with silence to some pressing normative issues. Why should such avowed incompleteness—entailing failure to sat-

77. For a general characterization of counterexamples that can be directed at most of the theories currently prominent, see Fishkin, *Tyranny and Legitimacy.*

78. As Bernard Williams notes in his critique, one of utilitarianism's distinctive aspirations is to answer virtually any moral problem so "it will have something to say even on the difference between massacring seven million, and massacring seven million and one." Bernard Williams, "A Critique of Utilitarianism," in J. J. C. Smart and Bernard Williams, *Utilitarianism: For and Against* (Cambridge: Cambridge University Press, 1973), p. 93. However, as Williams notes (p. 135), the original chosen ground for utilitarianism was social and political decision. And the defects of the theory for individual choice can be distinguished from those arising in social choice, as Williams's own argument from "integrity" attests.

isfy expectation 3—de-legitimate the theory for the range of cases that it *does* presume to deal with?[79] Until some convincing affirmative answer is offered to this question, I will assume that mere incompleteness (short of such pervasive silence as to render a theory trivial in its prescriptions) is not, by itself, fatal to claims to objective validity. In any case, the theories mentioned exemplify the possibility of a middle ground between theories that conform to expectation 3, on the one hand, and theories that are subjectivist or relativist, on the other.

A similar point can be made about expectation 4. The liberal theories of justice filling out the middle ground in our scheme fall far short of being strictly neutral between all alternative possible moral perspectives and initial assumptions.[80] It should be obvious that these moral decision procedures, in themselves, constitute particular embodiments of the moral point of view, embodiments that constitute controversial rivals, one to another. Commitment to any one of them can be impugned as less than strictly neutral when the claims of rival procedures are taken into account. Furthermore, in order for these procedures to yield substantive implications, they have to incorporate some particular preferred interpretation of interests or relevant claims. In doing so, they cannot remain strictly neutral between alternative moral perspectives and initial assumptions.[81] The general point is that the perspective of such a completely unbiased observer, if it were to be strictly neutral, would be deprived of any substantive basis for choice. In any case, none of the theories illustrating the middle ground aspires to such a demanding degree of neutrality. Once again, these

79. For an example of such an explicitly incomplete theory see my account of nontyranny in part 1 of *Tyranny and Legitimacy*.

80. Ackerman's theory aspires to "neutrality" only in a more limited sense—neutrality between theories of the good and between persons themselves (no claims of superiority). The strict neutrality of expectation 4 applies to all alternative possible moral perspectives and initial assumptions.

81. For this argument developed in greater detail with respect to both Rawls and Ackerman see my "Can There Be a Neutral Theory of Justice?" and, with respect to Rawls, my "Justice and Rationality."

theories illustrate how one could fail to satisfy one of the expectations, but, nevertheless, lay claim to at least a minimal kind of objective validity.

A similar point can be made about the fifth expectation. There is no presumption that these moral decision procedures will yield results that conform to all conscientious moral opinions. In fact, the hypothetical character of these procedures is, precisely, a strategy for abstracting from the bases for conscientious moral disagreement in the actual world. Our actual moral disagreements are fueled by the biases of socialization, special pleading, and self-deception. The appeal of hypothetical moral decision procedures lies in the attempt to surmount these barriers to conscientious moral agreement by relegating the problem to a thought experiment where only the truly relevant factors can apply and where the sources of actual moral disagreement can be brought under control.[82] Once more, nonfulfillment of one of the expectations is a defining characteristic of these theories.

The sixth expectation raises more complex issues. The liberal theories of justice discussed here can all be interpreted as conforming to strict impartiality, that is, they determine moral requirements with no special regard for the agent's interests, situation, or relations with others. However, they need not determine *individual obligations* with strict impartiality so as to yield overload problems. Recall that the chosen ground of all these theories of justice—Rawls's theory, utilitarianism, Ackerman's theory, Dworkin's theory, and the other variants cited earlier—is *social* choice and in particular the distribution of goods and the design of institutions in a just society.[83] If the foundation in impartiality is restricted to this chosen ground, then overload for individuals may be avoided. This can be accomplished by a two-tiered strategy in which strict impartiality

82. This aspiration is clearest in Rawls, *A Theory of Justice*, pp. 118– 22, 136–42.
83. Note the qualifications to this claim in n. 78 above.

applies to the design of social institutions in a just society—yielding, indirectly, individual obligations to uphold the results of this social choice. But the route from strict impartiality directly to the obligations of each isolated individual would not be employed in this two-tiered strategy. Individuals may be insulated from an overload of obligations by social institutions that enforce more perfect moral cooperation, making sure that everyone does his share. And if everyone does his share, then the seemingly irresistible route to overload, in which each isolated individual is forced, too quickly, to take on all the burdens of the world, can be avoided.

Note that in individual choice, as opposed to social choice, we commonly give priority, at least on occasion, to moral requirements that run afoul of strict impartiality. This can be seen from the standard distinction between special and general obligations. Some obligations are based on a special history of relations among the parties or on particular roles voluntarily accepted by one of the parties. I have obligations to particular persons based on consent, promises, or contracts. These are all *special obligations* limited to the parties involved. By contrast, *general obligations* are not based on the particular history of relations or roles occupied by those involved. They apply among total strangers as much as they apply among close relations. The basic idea is that a general obligation is one that would be unaffected by exchanging the identity of the agent and the identity of the recipients (those to whom the obligation is owed) with those of any other persons who could fit the situation. We need not explore all the complexities of the distinction here.[84] The basic notion is a familiar one. My obligations to my mother are special. My obligations to contribute money to save starving refugees are general. They hold between total strangers, and if the particular identities of the agent and the recipients were changed, the obligations would remain unaffected.

84. See Fishkin, *The Limits of Obligation*, section 5, for some further refinements in this notion of general obligation.

The relevance of this distinction here is that it brings into relief priorities that could not be sustained with strict impartiality. Charles Fried posed the problem of whether, in a lifeboat situation in which only one person could be saved, a rescuer would have to flip a coin in order to be suitably impartial between saving his wife and saving a total stranger.[85] Only if a moral position were designed so that special obligations could never override general ones could such an issue appear as a problem. Similarly, what troubled our ordinary reasoners in the famine relief case was the problem of giving some priority to members of their own family and others "close" to them. Because the effort to do so appeared unjustifiable from any strictly impartial moral perspective applied directly to individual choice, they chose to abandon impartiality and maintain the priority for those close to them. If, however, they had formulated the claim of those close to them as a conflicting moral obligation, as a special rather than general obligation, they might have found a moral basis for their preferences.

If strict impartiality is restricted to social choice and the design of social institutions, there may be room, within a two-tiered strategy of justification, for a high priority to be given to the practices defining many special obligations. Obligations to family members, obligations to keep contracts and promises, may achieve higher priority when they are placed within a framework of just social institutions.[86] If strict impartiality is applied to this framework rather than to the acts of individuals taken in isolation, then it may leave room for the familiar special obligations as a high priority. This high priority would

85. Charles Fried, *An Anatomy of Values* (Cambridge, Mass.: Harvard University Press, 1970), p. 227. See the critique by Bernard Williams, *Moral Luck* (Cambridge: Cambridge University Press, 1981), p. 17.

86. The point is parallel to familiar rule-utilitarian arguments for such institutions or social practices. See J. O. Urmson, "The Interpretation of the Moral Philosophy of J. S. Mill," Jonathan Harrison, "Utilitarianism, Universalization and Our Duty to Be Just," and John Rawls "Two Concepts of Rules," all in Michael D. Bayles, ed., *Contemporary Utilitarianism* (New York: Anchor Press, 1968).

appear unsupportable if strict impartiality is applied directly to the determination of individual obligations among persons considered in isolation.

For my purposes here, I do not need to argue the correctness of a priority for some special obligations (under at least some conditions), or of the two-tiered strategy with which it can be supported. I only need argue that the resulting position is a *possible* alternative, one that illustrates how primacy can be given to impartiality—but in a way that avoids the disturbing implications for individual obligation we encountered in the overload argument. We can, in other words, reject strict impartiality as a requirement applied directly to individual obligations without also having to adopt subjectivism.

This family of liberal theories of justice shows how subjectivism can be avoided, but it does not show that it must be. These theories are distinctive because they fill out, in rigorous fashion, an alternative route that can be taken after lack of the characteristics specified by the six expectations is admitted. From the perspective of our scheme there is no need to conclude, merely from the rejection of a demanding version of position I (labeled Kantian-absolutism in section 4.1), that we have no alternative but to choose one of the subjectivist positions (IV, V, VI, or VII). We still have remaining position III and, in some cases, position II as viable alternatives. Since our ordinary reasoners felt trapped in subjectivism by the logic of their rejection of absolutism, the distinctions embodied in the scheme of alternatives constitute a useful antidote to this move—a move that was adopted because there seemed to have been no alternative.

However, subjectivist reasoners can consistently maintain their positions—and the rigor of their arguments for those positions—by refusing to admit the middle-ground alternatives as objective possibilities at all. If they cling to the absolutist expectations that are a familiar part of our moral culture, then their case for subjectivism is virtually inescapable.

I do not aim to refute subjectivism. It remains a possibility, but not one that is inescapable—provided that our scheme of ethical positions is accepted as an account of the alternative possibilities. My aim is to show that once the measure of truth in subjectivist arguments is granted, there is still room for positions that provide morality with a basis that is not entirely "arbitrary," not entirely "subjective." If we attribute such a basis to at least some of our moral judgments, then we are claiming that they are more than arbitrary personal tastes. We are claiming that others, were they to consider the problem in a reasonable manner from what we regard as the appropriate perspective, would come to the same conclusions. The moral decision procedures that provide the basis for recent liberal theories of justice formalize these notions of an appropriate moral perspective and of reasonable choice within it. Yet whenever we appeal to others to look at a moral problem from a fair perspective, to abstract from their own interests by putting themselves in the shoes of other people, we are employing, at least implicitly, some such notion of reasonable choice from an appropriately impartial moral perspective.

To deny even this minimal claim, to embrace subjectivism by regarding even one's most fundamental principles as arbitrary personal tastes, as unsupportable personal preferences, is to open the door to another set of difficulties. Just as the consideration of objective alternatives in our scheme shows how subjectivism can be avoided, a consideration of the subjective alternatives in the scheme reveals further arguments for doing so. Each of the subjective possibilities in the scheme encounters difficulties that, together, make the entire route of escape from objectivism less plausible and less attractive than might appear at first glance.

In choosing among positions IV, V, VI, and VII, a potential subjectivist faces the difficulty that he must choose either a position that arbitrarily imposes preferences upon others or one that renders dubious the sense in which he can retain his values, recognizably, as moral values at all. Of course, if he wishes, he can obfuscate the issue or avoid facing it by relinquishing the attempt to develop any explicit position at all. But any subjectivist who attempts to spell out his position on these meta-ethical issues must face some portion or other of this subjectivist's dilemma.

The problem of arbitrarily "imposing" preferences on others applies to any variant of position IV, subjective universalism. In many cases, realization of this problem seems to drive our reasoners to the more extreme subjectivist positions. They avoid imposing their admittedly subjective preferences on others by becoming relativists, personalists, or amoralists. Recall Sam's comparison of his most cherished values ("honesty" is an example) with his preferences for food: "I prefer a T-bone steak to a sirloin because we used to have T-bones instead of sirloins. In the same sense, I grew up and developed a taste for honesty. That's as far as I can take it." It seems inappropriate to "impose" those values on others, once they are assimilated to this model of personal tastes. Even in the case of the hated druggist in the Heinz dilemma Sam says: "I think it would be very unfair to impose upon the druggist the valuation or the idea that he has to value Mrs. Heinz's life over his own satisfaction." Sam limits his judgments of others, even of the druggist, to those offered from their respective "perspectives" or "points of view."

Stephen's personalism, as we saw earlier, was also based on a concern for not "imposing" or "dictating" values to others, no matter how intensely he felt about those values himself. Nancy expressed a similar concern: "I'm not God and I can't go around saying what other people's values are . . . or should be." Similarly, Tom's fracturing of moral judgments from different perspectives and "points of view" is motivated by an effort to avoid "dictating" to others. "In a given situation," he says, "there is more than one way to act morally." Although he regards this diversity of prescriptions as "disconcerting," he concludes: "I mean the alternative is to say, 'this is right' and 'this is wrong,' and ultimately that's an autocratic system—this has been dictated as right and this has been dictated as wrong."

The underlying issue troubling these reasoners is that once they admit that their values are merely arbitrary personal tastes, it seems "autocratic," dictatorial, or a matter of "imposing" to apply them to those who disagree. Following their frequent comparison of these values to preferences for food, it would seem autocratic or dictatorial for Sam to impose his preference for T-bone steaks rather than sirloins on those who had contrary preferences. Since he has already come to regard his moral values (such as his "taste for honesty") as no more justifiable or supportable than his taste for T-bone steaks, in adopting relativism he has done no more than apply to morality the same consideration for contrary preferences he would apply to tastes for food. In admitting that his values are "tastes" he is placing them in a category where imposing his preferences on those who disagree seems inappropriate. He is admitting, in effect, that he does not have a basis for imposing them where tastes differ—but subjective universalism would require precisely that.

Why does subjective universalism require the imposition of preferences on those who disagree? A universalizable judgment has the form, "Anyone should (or should not) do X under conditions C." Even if we were to adopt the controversial move of including a condition such as "the person required to perform the action (or not to perform it) should agree that he should do so (or not do so)" within our account of the conditions C, we would *still* be committed to cases of arbitrary imposition. We would be committed to a host of prescriptions based on no more than admittedly arbitrary personal taste—prescriptions that would conflict with the values of others. Anyone who evaluated whether a person should do X on different grounds than our specification of C would be judged wrong by our principle. The form of universalizable consistency, by itself, carries with it implications for how everyone should judge whether X should be performed. In other words, even if we attempted to construct a universalizable principle that went far beyond any plausible concessions in the direction of not requiring others to act when they disagreed, we would still be committed to the imposition of preferences that were admitted to be nothing more than arbitrary. Of course, most familiar specifications of C above would not include any riders about the agreement of others. Hence such familiar versions of universalizable principles would include many more cases of arbitrary imposition—since anyone would be required to do X (or not do X) whether or not he agreed he should.

A defender of subjective universalism might reply that if all moral judgments are arbitrary, then this squeamishness about imposing arbitrary preferences on those who disagree is, in itself, a moral requirement that lacks any basis, just like any other moral requirement. However, the issue is not the basis for one moral requirement compared with another, since the subjectivist admits that there can be no such basis in any case. The issue, rather, is the plausibility of the subjectivist's interpretation of the phenomenon of morality. In denying claim 3, objective validity, subjectivists assimilate moral judgments to the model of personal tastes or arbitrary preferences. The difficulty confronting the subjective universalist, the proponent of position IV in particular, is that the model of personal tastes, at least as commonly understood, includes understandings about the interpersonal application of those preferences—and those understandings are incompatible with subjective universalism.

The incompatibility with subjective universalism arises for cases of arbitrary imposition. The subjective universalist, in adopting the model of personal "tastes" or unsupported "preferences," faces the problem that as a subjective universalist he must impose those preferences on others who disagree—even though the model of personal tastes to which he has assimilated moral judgments does not, as normally understood, apply in that way. Sam feels squeamish about imposing his "taste" for honesty universally precisely because he would not impose his taste for T-bone steaks in that way. The imposition of values on those with contrary preferences would seem to require some justification. It shifts the burden of proof onto those who would do the imposing. The difficulty, as our subjectivists are all too aware, is that their generally subjective positions rule out any justification responding to this burden of proof. They cannot respond to this burden of proof precisely because they are subjectivists.

Although our subjective universalists may, with logical consistency, maintain their positions, they cannot do so by simply adopting the model of arbitrary personal tastes or preferences. They must revise that model so as to permit an application of their values to others—an application that imposes preferences on others while at the same time acknowledging that those preferences are purely subjective. They can, if they wish, accept these "autocratic" or "dictatorial" implications, but the position seems far less plausible, and less attractive as an alternative, when revised in this way.

The remaining subjectivist positions—relativism, personalism, and amoralism—avoid this problem of arbitrary imposition but at the cost of rendering their values difficult to construe as moral values at all. In sacrificing universalizability, interpersonal judgment, and even judgment of self, they are sacrificing conditions that are basic constitutive features of the moral character of their positions.

First, consider the relativist. The relativist can avoid arbitrary imposition by regarding the values of others as providing both the necessary and sufficient conditions for their evaluating and performing the actions in question. Unlike the subjective universalist, the relativist can also avoid prescribing that others judge actions by *his* (the relativist's) values. In violating universalizability, he acknowledges that he is committed to differing evaluations of the same act from differing "points of view." If the differentiations provided by conflicting points of view are carefully maintained, then it may be possible to preserve logical consistency in the resulting position. "From my point of view X was wrong" and "From his point of view X was right" are logically compatible statements. But they become statements about the preferences or points of view of specifiable individuals rather than about the attributes of the prescribed actions—

attributes that would remain unchanged regardless of the perspective or point of view of the evaluation.

Something central to morality is lost by this effort to render relativism logically consistent—by this effort to specify the point of view or perspective from which a judgment is offered so that apparently conflicting judgments are always differentiable as statements about different points of view on the same action. The difficulty is that the very problem of moral disagreement that helps drive reasoners to relativism becomes impossible even to state once the position is construed consistently in this way. If I say "X is right," and you say, "X is wrong," we think we are disagreeing about something. But, as already noted, these statements are logically compatible once they are interpreted as "From my perspective X is right" and "From your perspective X is wrong." They become reports on the attributes of perspectives or points of view rather than statements about the attributes of the action X. In relinquishing universalizability so as to avoid arbitrary imposition, relativists render moral disagreements, as we commonly understand them, impossible even to state.

Can the possibility of stating moral disagreements be reintroduced by some modification of relativism? Efforts to reintroduce it run afoul of the relativist's concern to avoid unjustified imposition. For example, if we were to interpret A's statement "X is right" and B's statement "X is wrong" as "X is right from A's perspective and should be from B's as well" and "X is wrong from B's perspective and should be from A's as well," we would be reintroducing a kind of moral disagreement in attitude—but at the cost of prescriptions for others that violate the strictures of relativism and that also reintroduce the problem of arbitrary imposition: A is prescribing judgments for B who disagrees, even though A also admits that he has no basis to do so but subjective preference.

The problem is a variation of the old one that troubled C. L. Stevenson. If one reduces "This is good" to "I approve of this," then ethical disagreements become impossible even to state. "I approve of this" and "You don't approve of this" are not incompatible statements, even though "This is good" and "This is bad" are thought to be incompatible. However, if one adds prescriptions for others to bare expressions of approval and disapproval, as in Stevenson's working model for "This is good"—"I approve of this; do so as well"—the problem we have called arbitrary imposition of preferences on others surfaces again precisely because each moral judgment then carries implications for others (that is, "Do so as well"). The following statements, in other words, are incompatible, but only because they presume to impose their admittedly arbitrary prescriptions on others:

A. I approve of this; do so as well.
B. No, I disapprove of it; do so as well.[87]

The same issue arises for Gilbert Harman's recent efforts to reformulate relativism. Harman's relativism offers a dramatic example of the difficulties, within relativism, of stating fundamental moral disagreements. Harman's thesis applies to what he calls "inner judgments, such as the judgment that someone ought or ought not to have acted in a certain way or the judgment that it was right or wrong of him to have done so."[88] All such judgments, Harman believes, are "relative" to an "agreement or understanding." Without such an understanding, we have no basis for applying an inner judgment. So, in the dra-

87. C. L. Stevenson, *Ethics and Language* (New Haven: Yale University Press, 1944), p. 22. For a critique of Stevenson's models see J. O. Urmson, *The Emotive Theory of Ethics* (London: Hutchinson University Library, 1968), chaps. 4–6.
88. Gilbert Harman, "Moral Relativism Defended," *The Philosophical Review* 84, no. 1 (January 1975): 4. Harman says on the same page that his thesis is about "logical form" and not about the "objectivity" of morality. However, he continues the discussion in greater detail in his book *The Nature of Morality* (New York: Oxford University Press, 1977), where he offers it as part of his argument for a "moderate" version of "nihilism" (which, in our terms, would imply a denial of objective validity).

matic case of Hitler, Harman concludes: "To say, 'It was wrong of Hitler' or 'Hitler ought morally not to have done it' would imply that Hitler accepted the relevant moral conventions. But his actions show that he does not accept those conventions."[89] Harman explains:

> The inner judgments sound too weak not because of the enormity of what Hitler did but because we suppose that in acting as he did he shows that he could not have been susceptible to the moral considerations on the basis of which we make our judgment. He is in the relevant sense beyond the pale and we therefore cannot make inner judgments about him.[90]

If we abide by Harman's theory restricting the application of inner judgments to those who subscribe to the relevant agreements or understandings, we cannot even state our dramatic moral disagreement with Hitler and the Nazis about whether they ought to have exterminated millions of Jews. We cannot apply the inner judgment to them that they ought to have acted otherwise. And if their acts conform to their own understandings and conventions, they can support the conclusion that they were required to act in that way, without our having any basis, within Harman's theory, for disputing the conclusion. Of course, we can hope or wish that they had adopted different conventions, we can argue that *their* values really prescribe different actions,[91] and we can judge that, as persons, they were "evil" (for that is not an inner judgment).[92] But we are restricted even from prescribing to the Nazis that they should have acted otherwise if we conform to the relativistic logical form of inner judgments advocated by Harman—provided that the Nazis act consistently on the basis of their *own* moral agreements and

89. Harman, *The Nature of Morality*, p. 109.
90. Harman, "Moral Relativism," p. 7.
91. See "Moral Relativism," p. 16, and *The Nature of Morality*, p. 97, for some of these possibilities.
92. *The Nature of Morality*, p. 125.

understandings. Hence, Harman's variation of relativism, like other versions, would render some of our most fundamental moral disagreements impossible even to state.

The basic problem facing all these subjectivist positions is that if the subjectivist interprets his moral values as applying to others who disagree, he faces the problem of arbitrary imposition. But if he does not interpret them as applying to others who disagree, then he is without any means even of stating fundamental moral disagreements. Obviously, consistent versions of personalism and amoralism only render the possibility of stating moral disagreements more difficult. The personalist's values cannot, even in theory, entangle him in moral disagreements about the behavior of others. And the amoralist does not have any values that he regards as moral values at all.

Even more than the relativist, the personalist and amoralist positions render dubious the sense in which the agent has any recognizably moral values. This conclusion is obvious in the case of the amoralist, who has explicitly relinquished his claim to any moral position. In the personalist's case, his values lack both universalizable and interpersonal application. If he judges an action wrong or right, it is wrong or right only for him and not for others, even when they are in apparently similar circumstances. If he ventures to make any prescriptions for others, he has departed from the boundaries of personalism (into relativism or subjective universalism, for example). Within these boundaries the value judgments remaining to him are arbitrarily tied to his identity as a moral agent. They have been reduced to *sui generis* statements about *him*, applicable to no one else. They are no longer statements about kinds of human action, since if they were, they would be performable by others, at least in theory. It is difficult to recognize in the personalist's position the features of a morality, since the personalist's judgments do not apply to actions that are available to be performed, even in theory, by anyone else. If moral prescriptions must classify at least some kinds of human action that are generally available, then the personalist's position falls short of this requirement.

The problem of moral disagreement (and the lack of any sufficiently firm basis for resolving it) has fueled several of the arguments for subjectivism (particularly the first argument). Alternatively, the problem of imposing values on those who conscientiously disagree has yielded us the fifth argument. Although these two problems provide much of the motivation for subjectivism in the first place, consistent versions of subjectivism do not succeed in resolving them. Subjective universalism remains vulnerable to the problem of arbitrary imposition. Relativism, personalism, and amoralism provide us with positions that render fundamental moral disagreements impossible even to state. In addition, they provide us with positions that lack, in increasingly extreme ways, the defining character of moral positions. The subjectivist's dilemma is that, in choosing a position, he must either accept arbitrary imposition (at position IV) or render dubious the sense in which he has a moral position at all (at positions V, VI, or VII).

When these difficulties applying to the various versions of subjectivism are added to the avoidability of subjectivism (via the middle ground outlined earlier), the previously irresistible force of subjectivist arguments can be defused.

The middle ground developed here has the twofold merit that it does justice to the force of the subjectivist arguments against fulfillment of the six expectations while it also avoids both horns of the subjectivist dilemma. It does not commit us to cases of admittedly unjustified imposition nor does it render fundamental moral disagreements impossible to formulate. These theoretical merits of the middle ground do not amount to, and are not in any way intended as, a demonstration that it is ultimately correct—that, specifically, some minimal objectivist interpretation of morality is true. But these merits do show how, if we can learn to expect less of an objective morality, we can reasonably endow our most cherished convictions with the seriousness they have always appeared to require. Claims to moral reasonableness in this sense are not beyond dispute. But that does not show that they are entirely beyond reason.

4.6. What Is Moral Development?

Thus far, my argument has two main components. First, we cannot reasonably expect to arrive at positions fulfilling the requirements of the six expectations. This is the half-truth underlying the subjectivist arguments of ordinary reasoners. Second, subjectivism is avoidable, even when nonfulfillment of these expectations is granted, because there are various middle-ground positions that provide alternatives to subjectivism, even though they fail to fulfill the six expectations.

This argument has implications not only for meta-ethical issues about the foundations of morality but also for the philosophical issues applying to Kohlberg's theory of moral development. Kohlberg's basic philosophical claims for his higher stages are that they fulfill many of the Kantian-absolutist expectations discussed here. He claims the "higher" stages are "better" precisely because they have these valued characteristics. Such philosophical contentions are central to the theory, if movement to the higher stages is to be considered "moral development."

Kohlberg's "Platonic" assumption—"that he who knows the good chooses the good"—commits him to fulfillment of expectations 1 and 5 (that his resolutions are beyond reasonable question and conform to conscientious moral opinion). The hypothesis is ruled out that someone could truly understand a higher stage and also reject it:

> If the higher stage solution is "seen," it is preferred to the lower stage solution, whatever the particular experiences with either stage solution. This is because part of seeing the higher stage is seeing why it is better than the lower stage solution.[93]

93. Lawrence Kohlberg, "Continuities in Childhood and Adult Moral Development Revisited," in P. B. Baltes and K. W. Schnie, eds., *Life-Span*

Kohlberg holds moral knowledge to be beyond reasonable question in a way analogous to our knowledge of geometry: "The Platonic view implies that, in a sense, knowledge of the good is always within but needs to be drawn out like geometric knowledge in Meno's slave."[94]

The highest stages would then satisfy the first expectation. They would also satisfy the second expectation (inviolability) because stages 5 and 6 both consist in "principles" rather than "rules." According to Kohlberg, a defining characteristic of principles is that they are inviolable:

> By a moral principle we mean a mode of choosing which is universal, a rule of choosing which we want all people to adopt in all situations . . . There are exceptions to rules but *no exceptions to principles* [italics added].[95]

Stage 6 would also satisfy the third expectation since it purports to be complete. Kohlberg says of stage 6: "The claim of principled morality is that it *defines the right for anyone in any situation*" [italics added].[96] It does this by being more "differentiated" than preceding stages. For example, for every valid claim to a "right" at stage 6 there is a "correlative" determination of a "duty." By contrast, Kohlberg believes stage 5 to be inadequate because its rights and duties are "not completely correlative." This means that some duties "are not completely specified" at stage 5. At stage 6, however, this indeterminacy is remedied by making everyone's duties duties and rights completely correlative.[97]

Furthermore, Kohlberg's stage 6 applies strict impartiality directly to the determination of individual obligation. Although Kohlberg regards stage 6 as equivalent to Rawls's theory of

Developmental Psychology: Personality and Socialization (New York: Academic Press, 1973), p. 194.

94. Kohlberg, "Education for Justice: a Modern Statement of the Platonic View," in T. Sizer, ed., *Moral Education: Five Lectures* (Cambridge, Mass.: Harvard University Press, 1970), p. 80.

95. Ibid., p. 69.

96. Kohlberg, "From Is to Ought," p. 185.

97. Lawrence Kohlberg, "The Claim to Moral Adequacy of a Highest Stage of Moral Development," *Journal of Philosophy* 70 (1973):630–46.

justice for social choice, he extends the idea explicitly and directly to individual obligation. In what he calls "moral musical chairs," the Golden Rule is applied by each person changing places with every other. When my changing places with every other person produces the same solution as that yielded by every other person changing places with every other, then we have an "equilibrated" stage 6 solution. Since every person's "right" to be helped produces a "correlative duty" that he be helped, the route to overload, particularly in a world of imperfect moral cooperation, is straightforward and direct.[98]

Although this picture of morality is undoubtedly appealing, it encounters all the difficulties discussed earlier. The Platonic assumption does not do justice to the room for conscientious and reasonable moral disagreement we encountered in the jurisdiction problem. The requirements that principles be inviolable and that they resolve every question do not do justice to the moral complexities we encountered in the foreseeability problem. And the requirement of strict impartiality embodied in "moral musical chairs" yields an overload of individual obligations for large-scale social problems.

If my arguments against fulfillment of these expectations have been correct, then what Kohlberg calls moral development is not development at all, for it is not movement to a more adequate moral position. In fact, our subjectivist reasoners, in realizing the difficulties with these requirements, are in some sense more developed than those who move to Kohlberg's higher stages. Our subjectivist reasoners have, at least, come to terms with the true complexity and room for reasonable controversy applying to morality.

Of course, our subjectivist reasoners have not arrived at adequate positions either. They face the subjectivist's dilemma

98. Kohlberg, *The Philosophy of Moral Development*, vol. 1, chap. 5, "Justice as Reversibility." Each person's right to be helped produces a correlative duty that he be helped. If there is imperfect moral cooperation so that others do not all do their share, then so long as I would require action after trading places with those who would be helped (Kohlberg's "musical chairs" version of the Golden Rule), I am obligated to do so.

outlined earlier, and their rationales for subjectivism eliminate or ignore the middle ground advocated here. The middle-ground positions would not be classified highly by Kohlberg because they do not fulfill the requirements for stage 6 (and sometimes even the requirements for stage 5) in being inviolable, complete and beyond reasonable question (in the sense of Kohlberg's Platonic assumption). Yet if these middle ground positions are more adequate to the complexity and controversiality of morality, then there is a sense in which they constitute meta-ethical development—compared with the simplifications of stage 6 expectations on the one hand and the overreactions of complete subjectivism on the other.

4.7. The Cultural Crisis of Liberalism

In section 4.2 I distinguished internal and external strategies of justification. An internal strategy is based on assumptions internal to the characterization of morality or the moral point of view. An external strategy, on the other hand, is based on assumptions independent of the characterization of morality or the moral point of view itself—assumptions, for example, about God, metaphysics, or the role of humanity in the universe.

At earlier stages in the development of liberalism, there may have been enough of a religious and metaphysical consensus to support external strategies of argument with enough conclusiveness to satisfy (or appear to satisfy) absolutist expectations. As John Dunn has shown, the religious assumptions crucial to Locke's *Two Treatises* were "rigidly conventional" and widely shared; they were a "common backcloth" available in the culture providing a shared foundation for argument.[99] A similar point can be made about the God-given natural rights, the "self-evident" truths appealed to by the American founding fathers.[100]

99. John Dunn, *The Political Thought of John Locke: An Historical Account of the Argument of the "Two Treatises of Government"* (Cambridge: Cambridge University Press, 1969), p. 88.
100. Morton White, *The Philosophy of the American Revolution* (New York: Oxford University Press, 1978), chap. 4.

However, this religious and metaphysical consensus is not available to contemporary liberal theorists in the same way. Science has undermined crucial religious and metaphysical claims.[101] Furthermore, the ethnic and cultural diversity of modern pluralistic societies brings disagreement about religious and metaphysical assumptions into sharper relief.

It is also true that were a state to base itself today on the controversial religious or metaphysical assumptions of any particular group, that would in itself seem illiberal: it would lack the minimal degree of *neutrality* required by a liberal state on such matters. Particularly in the United States, where the separation of church and state has given rise to an elaborate doctrine of state neutrality,[102] the state could not enshrine the religious convictions of any particular group by public commitments and avoid the charge that it was biasing the marketplace of ideas by giving certain religious and metaphysical claims, certain ultimate convictions, the stamp of state authority and legitimacy.

By "ultimate convictions" here I mean religious or metaphysical assumptions on fundamental issues that might provide an external basis for morality. Our cherished beliefs about God, about the purpose of human creation, about the goal of history, about the possible character of an afterlife, offer familiar examples of such ultimate convictions. It would be out of bounds for a liberal state to base moral arguments—and, in particular, to base its own claims to legitimacy—on the ultimate convictions of any particular group. Any state that did so would not preserve the minimum degree of neutrality that must characterize a liberal state. Although this external strategy of

---

101. For a brief account of some of these conflicts, both apparent and real, see Paul Roubiczek, *Ethical Values in the Age of Science* (Cambridge: Cambridge University Press, 1969), part 1. A more ambitious statement can be found in Thomas A. Spragens, Jr., *The Irony of Liberal Reason* (Chicago: University of Chicago Press, 1981).

102. For an influential statement see Philip B. Kurland, *Religion and the Law: Of Church and State and the Supreme Court* (Chicago: Aldine, 1962).

justification might be available to the Ayatollah Khomeini or to King Fahd of Saudi Arabia, it would not be available in a liberal state. We now realize that theocratic solutions are sufficiently un-neutral as to be illiberal. While this seems, in many ways, a special merit of liberalism, it renders liberalism vulnerable to subjectivism, in a way that other ideologies (those not requiring this kind of neutrality) may escape.

If this account of the minimum degree of neutrality necessary for liberal theory is correct, then external strategies of justification are not available to contemporary liberalism. But the alternative general category of internal strategies (whether deductive or inductive[103]) will, as we have already seen from our discussion of the jurisdiction problem, produce only inconclusive results.

I have tried to argue that this inconclusiveness need not be fatal to objective claims for liberalism. However, my arguments have depended on rejection of the six expectations as necessary conditions for objective validity. Whether or not I am correct in this meta-ethical argument, these expectations pose a crucial *cultural* problem for the viability of liberalism as a coherent moral ideology. For, as we have seen, external strategies of justification are unavailable to liberal theory. But internal strategies of justification can be expected to yield no more than inconclusiveness. Once this inconclusiveness is combined with absolutist expectations that have wide currency in the culture, a logically unavoidable and obvious route to subjectivism has been created. Furthermore, this route to subjectivism applies not merely to the moral positions of isolated individuals but also to whatever moral position can be attributed to the liberal state itself. In a moral and political culture imbued with absolutist expectations, the liberal state's own claims to legitimacy must be self-undermining, on close analysis. Liberalism is inevitably vulnerable to self-destruction

103. See n. 62 above.

as a coherent moral ideology in a culture imbued with such expectations, because the inevitable inconclusiveness of the internal strategies available must fall short of absolutist expectations.

Of course, the ordinary reasoners who gave testimony here about these absolutist expectations do not speak for our entire moral culture. But the sense of familiarity I think we all find in these arguments, the sense in which they are often so familiar as to seem like philosophical clichés, buttresses my claim that they constitute widely shared assumptions, a common cultural backdrop on meta-ethical questions. To whatever extent these assumptions are shared, they provide the fulcrum for shaking the foundations of liberalism—in the eyes of those who share those expectations and who draw the required logical implications.

Some familiar attacks on liberalism can be seen in this light as no more than applications to liberal theory of the same meta-ethical arguments our ordinary reasoners applied to their own positions. Leo Strauss, for example, attacked Isaiah Berlin's affirmation of conflicting, controversial principles as "a characteristic document in the crisis of liberalism—of a crisis due to the fact that liberalism has abandoned its absolutist basis and is trying to become entirely relativistic."[104] Similarly, Roberto Mangabeira Unger's polemic against liberalism depends on the claim that liberalism cannot avoid commitment to the "subjectivity of values" and, hence, that its claims to legitimacy must be self-undermining.[105]

I cannot begin to retrace the history of such attacks here. Rather, my purpose is to make an analytical point about the strategies available to liberal theory. Any version of liberal theory we might plausibly envisage cannot employ an external strategy so as to satisfy absolutist expectations. It cannot do so

104. Leo Strauss, "Relativism," in Helmut Schoek and James W. Wiggins, eds., *Relativism and the Study of Man* (Princeton: Van Nostrand, 1961), p. 140.
105. Roberto Mangabeira Unger, *Knowledge and Politics* (New York: Free Press, 1976), especially pp. 85–87.

because that would make the resulting state illiberal in its bias toward the controversial ultimate convictions of a portion of its citizens. Alternatively, internal strategies cannot be expected to satisfy absolutist expectations either. If the ground rules for an objective moral ideology are to be set by these expectations, then liberalism cannot be expected to satisfy them. But a moral ideology that is not objective—that supports claims to its own subjectivity or arbitrariness—strips itself of legitimacy and authority.[106] In that sense liberalism self-destructs as a coherent moral ideology in a culture imbued with such expectations.

In many ways this entire book can be read as a proposal for a change in moral culture—for a change in our common expectations about the character of an objective morality. Such a change would not only permit subjectivism to be avoided by individuals, it would also permit self-destruction, or self-delegitimation, to be avoided by liberal theory—through the theoretical availability of a middle ground.

But that availability is not merely theoretical. The availability of a nonsubjective morality to us will depend on how we choose to regard our most cherished convictions. In the end, we answer these meta-ethical questions not only by how we think about morality but also by how we live. If we reduce our most cherished convictions to subjectivism, to the model of arbitrary preferences, we are subscribing to a form of moral culture and to a form of life within it. My argument has been that although that form of life is a possible one, it is neither as plausible nor as inevitable as certain assumptions within our culture would lead us to believe. While I have not shown how subjectivism *must* be avoided, I have shown how it *may* be, if only we choose to think and to live in the manner required.

---

106. By this I mean *moral* legitimacy and authority. The Marxist strategy of basing claims to a kind of legitimacy on historical inevitability remains a possibility. It is, however, based on controversial assumptions and is not available to liberalism in the same way that it is available to Marxism. For a sympathetic account see G. A. Cohen, *Karl Marx's Theory of History: A Defense* (Princeton: Princeton University Press, 1978).

Appendix A: More on Kohlberg and the Empirical Study of Moral Reasoning

Kohlberg has made several bold claims about the stages in his theory. Most important are the following:

1. They form a universally "invariant sequence" despite "varying cultural conditions."[1]
2. They represent a "hierarchy of cognitive difficulty."[2]
3. They represent a "hierarchy of moral adequacy." The "higher" stages resolve ethical issues left unresolved by the lower stages.[3]
4. They represent a "hierarchy of perceived moral adequacy" such that agents (with the possible exception of those in disequilibrium between stages) always prefer the highest stage they understand.[4]
5. They represent "structured wholes" that are both more

1. Kohlberg, "From Is to Ought," p. 169. Recently Kohlberg has introduced one qualification, namely, that the sixth stage is no more than "a theoretical hypothesis." "Continuing empirical work," we are told, "has not allowed us to confirm the existence of, or define a sixth stage." See Lawrence Kohlberg, "A Reply to Owen Flanagan and Some Comments on the Puka-Goodpaster Exchange," *Ethics* 92, no. 3 (April 1982): 523.
2. Kohlberg, "From Is to Ought," p. 182.
3. Ibid., pp. 195–222. See also Lawrence Kohlberg, *Essays on Moral Development*, vol. 1 *The Philosophy of Moral Development: Moral Stages and the Idea of Justice*, especially chapter 5, "Justice as Reversibility: The Claim to Moral Adequacy of a Highest Stage of Moral Development" (New York: Harper and Row, 1981).
4. Kohlberg, "From Is to Ought," p. 182.

"consistent" and more "stable" than the disequilibrium involved in movement between stages.[5]

6. They represent a sequence of moral commitments to the highest stage that is fully comprehended. The basis for stage assignment is commitment to (or advocacy of) reasoning at a given stage rather than merely the ability to understand it.

Subjectivism (termed *relativism* in the Kohlberg literature) poses a challenge, in one way or another, to each of these claims.[6] At first, subjectivism was interpreted as a "retrogression" to the childlike reasoning of instrumental hedonism (stage 2), even though many of the same reasoners had been classified earlier at stage 4 or 5. However, unlike the variety of stage 2 reasoners encountered in the normal process of development (a stage whose incidence decreases substantially from age 10 onward),[7] these stage 2 reasoners had "not lost their earlier capacity to use stage 4 and stage 5 thinking."[8] Thus if they were to be interpreted as having retrogressed while nevertheless continuing to understand the higher stages which they had rejected, then not only would the "invariant sequence" claim (2, above) be disconfirmed, but the claim of

5. For the consistency claim see Lawrence Kohlberg, "Stage and Sequence: The Cognitive–Developmental Approach to Socialization," in David Goslin, ed., *Handbook of Socialization Theory and Research* (New York: Rand McNally, 1969), pp. 347–480, especially 388. For the stability claim see "From Is to Ought," p. 185; for the challenge to it posed by relativistic reasoning see Turiel, "Conflict and Transition."

6. Most obviously, invariant sequence (1) is contradicted if relativism is interpreted as a regression back to stage 2. The perceived moral adequacy claim (4) is undermined if subjects understand the higher stages and reject them. The consistency and stability claims for the stages (5) are undermined by evidence that relativism stabilizes. Commitment as the basis for stage assignment (6) no longer holds if subjects are classified as "latently" at their higher stage even though they advocate reasoning at a lower one. More on these issues below.

7. Lawrence Kohlberg and Richard Kramer, "Continuities and Discontinuities in Child and Adult Moral Development," *Human Development* 12 (1969): 104.

8. Ibid., p. 112.

"perceived moral adequacy" (4, above) would be disconfirmed as well.

On the other hand, if they were to be interpreted as remaining "latently at . . . [their] achieved higher moral stage,"[9] then, although invariant sequence would be preserved, the assumptions of both perceived moral adequacy (4) and stage assignment by commitment (6) would be sacrificed.

Kohlberg later attempted to avoid this dilemma by categorizing subjectivism as a phenomenon of transition or disequilibrium between stages 4 and 5.[10]

> The apparent stage 2 thinking of the longitudinal subjects was not actually a return to an earlier pattern of stage 2 thought used when they were younger, but was actually a pattern of thought used in the *transition from* conventional to principled reasoning. The thinking of the transitional relativists in our sample could best be characterized as stage 4 1/2, i.e., as a way of thinking which equated morality with stage 4 thought and then questioned the validity of morality, conceived in stage 4 terms [italics in original].[11]

Such a categorization, if it were empirically supported, could successfully avoid the dilemma mentioned above in which either assumptions 1 and 4 or 4 and 6 had to be sacrificed. For if these subjectivists, who appeared at first to be at stage 2, were really all at stage 4 1/2 and if they were 4 1/2 *after* they had been predominantly stage 4 (and not stage 5) and *before* they had been predominantly stage 5 (and not stage 4), then no disconfirmation of invariant sequence would have occurred (thus preserving assumption 1). Furthermore, if these subjects were at

9. Norma Haan, "Activism as Moral Protest: Moral Judgments of Hypothetical and Actual Situations of Civil Disobedience," *The Development of Moral Judgment and Action*, ed. Lawrence Kohlberg and Elliot Turiel (New York: Holt, forthcoming).

10. Kohlberg, "Continuities in Childhood and Adult Moral Development Revisited," and Turiel, "Conflict and Transition."

11. Kohlberg, "Continuities in Childhood and Adult Moral Development Revisited," p. 22.

stage 4 1/2, it could then be claimed that they were in the process of working toward a more "equilibrated" and consistent position, so that if they failed to realize the greater "moral adequacy" of stage 5 compared with stage 4 (and 4 1/2 as well), such confusions could be permitted as characteristic of the brief transitional periods between stages. (Exceptions to assumption 4, the hierarchy of perceived adequacy, are permitted for subjects in transition.) Last, this hypothesis does not violate commitment as the basis for stage assignment (assumption 6), because these subjects had not been assigned to any given stage. Since they were in disequilibrium between stages, they could be expected to reject stage 4 while not accepting stage 5 but nevertheless to reason at roughly the level of competence of a premoral subject. Hence the problematical character of subjectivism for moral stage theory would appear to have been resolved.

However, this resolution depends on certain empirical claims that have not been established and that are in fact dubious in light of the existing evidence.

At least the following two claims would have to be established if subjectivists[12] were to be properly classified as experiencing a stage 4 1/2 transitional period:

a. It must be established that *4 1/2 follows stage 4 but not stage 5 or some other stage* (if assumption 1—invariant sequence—is to be preserved).

b. It must be established that *stage 5 follows 4 1/2 within a reasonable period* (if, according to assumption 5, transitional periods are to be distinguished from stages by their instability and by the fact that they lead to the next stage).[13]

12. The Kohlberg researchers refer to all these subjectivists as "relativists." As noted in chapter 2, I reserve this term for a subcategory of subjectivism (position V in my scheme). For a general characterization of subjectivist themes encountered among the Kohlberg "relativists" see Turiel, "Conflict and Transition," p. 19.

13. While transitional periods (by definition) lead to the next stage, stable stages may or may not be followed by the next stage.

One difficulty Kohlberg faced is that many of the original "retrogressors" were classified as having been at stage 5 before their reversion to instrumental hedonism—so many in fact that the pattern became known as the "5−2" or "Raskolnikov Regression."[14] If the stage 5 classifications were correct, then it would hardly be plausible to claim that *after* reaching stage 5 in high school these subjects displayed as sophomores in college the distinctive transitional characteristics of stage 4 1/2. One could not be in transition to a stage after it had been achieved unless the assumption of invariant sequence were to be relaxed.

This difficulty has been dealt with, however, by a "revised definition of the stages," which, we are told, more carefully distinguishes "structure" from "content."[15] As a result, Kohlberg concludes:

> The previous responses of these subjects which we had scored stage 5 were not really principled or stage 5. It was not really based upon principles or values which made sense from an "outside of society" perspective aware of the relativity of the particular rules of one's own society."[16]

In fact, given the strength of Kohlberg's commitment to the assumption of invariant sequence, he was willing to grant that: "The fact that the apparently stage 5 thinking of high school students was vulnerable to retrogression or was not yet fully stabilized was, in fact, evidence for the fact that such thinking was not really principled."[17]

However, even according to the revised stage definition, claim a above is subject to question. First, in an example of

14. For a summary of these initial conclusions by the Kohlberg researchers see Kenneth Keniston, "Student Activism, Moral Development and Morality," *American Journal of Orthopsychiatry* 40 (July 1970): 577−92, especially pp. 580−81. For details on stage 5 thinking by "regressives" see Kohlberg, "Continuities and Discontinuities," p. 106; and for an explanation of the "Raskolnikov" analogy, see p. 114.

15. Lawrence Kohlberg, "Continuities in Childhood and Adult Moral Development," pp. 36−37.

16. Ibid., p. 26.

17. Ibid., p. 20.

stage 5 that Kohlberg cites in the same article in which he proposes the stage revisions, the subject combines an argument for a stage 5 social contract with what, according to the latest criteria, may be characterized as a specifically stage 5 argument for the subjectivist claim that one should not "impose" value judgments on others. Based on what Kohlberg calls a stage 5 "recognition of the universality of the rights of other questioning selves," which is "reflected upon from some outside of society perspective,"[18] this subject argues that "I don't think I have a moral right to impose my moral standards on anyone else":

> Morality is a series of value-judgments. For me to say something is morally right means that in my own conscience, based on my experience and feelings, I would judge it right. But it is up to the individual, based on his individuality to determine if something is right, it need not be right all the time. I guess what I am saying is, *I don't think I have a moral right to impose my moral standards on anyone else.* Society, I think, mankind gets together in groups primarily for the good of themselves in general, but at the same time they then recognize that there is a certain benefit to do things for the good of society, according to a certain set of standards. Now these standards, of course, vary. Well, like it or not, Western society is based on some of the concepts of right and wrong, of the Judeo Christian teachings. What would society be without them? I think the one big keystone in this whole thing is what I go back to, the worth of the individual, an individual life is worth keeping and worth saving. It's like each life, each person has value to himself, to other people and to mankind as a whole [italics in original].[19]

To the extent that subjectivism can be explained at all in terms of "transitional" states *between* the Kohlberg stages, the subjectivism expressed by this subject, it might be argued, should be thought of as 5 1/2 rather than 4 1/2. I make this claim

18. Ibid., p. 28.
19. Ibid., p. 41.

not only because his other reasoning has been offered to us as an example of stage 5 but also because the basis for his subjectivist position appears to be a recognition of stage 5 universal rights valid "outside of society." His subjectivism would thus appear to take a characteristically stage 5 form just as the other transitional responses had a characteristically stage 4 form.

Similarly, to the extent that the responses of certain other subjectivists are to be understood within the framework of Kohlberg's stages (rather than within the alternative framework proposed here[20]), they might be more properly thought of as a subjectivist version of his stage 3 (and hence a position 3 1/2) than as a subjectivist version of stage 4 or 5. Kohlberg and Gilligan cite an unpublished study of California hippies by Haan and Holstein:

> The majority of a sample of Haight-Ashbury hippies emerge as mixtures of preconventional stage 2 and conventional stage 3 thinking. While hippie culture appears to be post-conventional, it is almost entirely a mixture of stage 2 "do your own thing" and stage 3 "be nice, be loving" themes. The hippie culture continually questions conventional morality but on stage 3 grounds of its being harsh and mean, or stage 2 grounds of "Why shouldn't I have fun?" rather than in terms of its irrationality.[21]

None of the revised criteria for stages would affect the specifically stage 3 grounds for the questioning of morality cited here.

However, the suggestion that there may be subjects in stages 3 1/2 and 5 1/2 as well as in Kohlberg's proposed 4 1/2 transitional phase does not, in principle, rule out Kohlberg's

20. I do not intend to resolve the questions at issue between the "transitional" and the "regression" hypotheses. Both approaches employ Kohlberg's normative-ethical paradigm. My proposal is a competing meta-ethical scheme intended to capture dimensions of moral reasoning misclassified by the Kohlberg scheme.

21. Lawrence Kohlberg and Carol Gilligan, "The Adolescent as a Philosopher: The Discovery of the Self in a Post-conventional World," *Daedalus* 100 (1971): 1051−86, especially 1080.

proposed explanation for subjectivism. A defender of Kohlberg's theory might argue that the "transitional" hypothesis be broadened to cover at least these three cases.[22] Therefore the difficulties we have discussed in claim a could be avoided if we reformulated it as follows:

> a': The transitional phase follows the stage that immediately precedes it in the hypothesized order, and not some other stage.

While this revision might resolve the problems concerning claim a, it would not similarly avoid major difficulties for claim b—a claim that would be equally essential for the "transitional" hypothesis. For subjectivism could hardly constitute a transitional period between stages unless it were not only preceded but also followed by the appropriate stages. Furthermore, the period of transition must be marked by less stability than that of an ordinary stage, otherwise it could plausibly be thought of as a distinctive stage in its own right.[23]

The second claim, therefore, would similarly have to be broadened as follows:

22. Since stages 1 and 2, in being preconventional, are also premoral, they would not produce transitional forms that relativize *moral* perspectives. Stage 6, on the other hand, is too rare to produce any characteristically transitional forms that might show up in the current literature. Hence we have limited speculation on the broadening of the "transitional" hypothesis to the only three remaining cases: 3 1/2, 4 1/2, 5 1/2.

23. Perry notes that it is standard practice in developmental theory to distinguish stages from transitional periods by their stability:

> The usual strategy for describing a developmental process . . . consists of taking cross sections at chosen intervals along the course of development . . . (when these cross sections are referred to as "stages") . . . the prior assumption is made that the development is not smooth and that the points of cross section have been dictated by a *differential in stability* evident in the forms making up the development. "Stages" then refer to relatively stable forms, and those less stable forms which mediate between stages are said to characterize "transitions" [italics in original].

William G. Perry, *Forms of Intellectual and Ethical Development in the College Years: A Scheme* (New York: Holt, Rinehart and Winston, 1968), p. 46.

b': The transitional phase is followed, within a reasonable period, by the stage that immediately follows it in the hypothesized order, and not by some other stage.

However, a major difficulty with claim b' results from the fact that although the Kohlberg and Kramer study of subjectivists in Kohlberg's original longitudinal sample initially confirmed the hypothesis that subjectivism was a short-lived phenomenon—one that was consistently followed by the subsequent stage[24]—more recent studies indicate that this pattern does not always hold with regularity. In particular, Kohlberg and Gilligan cite data collected by M. H. Podd leading them to the conclusion that subjectivism in the countercultural atmosphere of the late 1960s commonly proved to be a comparatively stable phenomenon:

> Extreme relativism no longer appeared to be a *temporary* ego-developmental maneuver of a small group of subjects in crisis, but rather to represent a more *stable*, less crisis-like pattern of low commitment [italics added].[25]

Writing in 1971, Kohlberg and Gilligan explain this new stability by citing the fact that subjectivism or "the relativistic rejection of convention . . . is now manufactured as a cultural industry called the 'counterculture.'" It has been "transform[ed] . . . into yet another conventional system."[26] As an alternative "conventional system" it should not be surprising if its stability proves comparable to that of the normal conventional stages.

In another article Kohlberg similarly qualifies the Kohlberg and Kramer conclusions with the claim that "there is no doubt that under some social conditions such [subjectivist] ideologies become stabilized orientations."[27] One such set of social conditions had been spelled out in an earlier analysis of

24. Kohlberg and Kramer, "Continuities and Discontinuities," p. 112.
25. Kohlberg and Gilligan, "The Adolescent as a Philosopher," p. 1080.
26. Ibid.
27. Kohlberg, "From Is to Ought," p. 204.

Adolf Eichmann's subjectivist statements, which led Kohlberg to conclude that patterns of stable subjectivism might develop within some political cultures.[28]

Yet if subjectivism can become a "stabilized orientation" under some sociocultural conditions, then, at least under those conditions, claim b' is falsified. This immediately suggests two lines of interpretation, either one of which would be equally fatal to the preservation of the original list of assumptions in its entirety. On the one hand, it might be claimed that subjectivism is not a transitional phenomenon but, in some sense, a conventional stage in its own right (as the Kohlberg and Gilligan article cited above appeared to suggest). However, this would mean that it was a stage involving no substantive *moral* commitment whatsoever (violating assumption 6) and, in that sense, a stage independent of the philosophical claims for normative adequacy advanced by assumption 3 and, perhaps, the empirical claim of perceived moral adequacy advanced by assumption 4. On the other hand, if it were claimed that despite its potential for stability, subjectivism is nevertheless a transitional phenomenon, then assumption 5 would be violated—for transitional periods, as phases of disequilibrium, must by definition be less stable (and less consistent) than the hypothesized stages.

Subjectivism thus constitutes a basic challenge to the root assumptions of the Kohlberg theory. This challenge derives from the fact that Kohlberg's classifications are primarily normative ethical but the phenomenon of subjectivism is essentially meta-ethical. There is no place within Kohlberg's scheme for meta-ethical questioning except in the gaps between stages. My position here is that once this misclassification is corrected, once explicitly meta-ethical classifications are employed, subjectivism can be seen not as a phase of inconsistency and confusion but rather as a position that subjects reach because it is more logically consistent and less confused than its alternatives—given the assumptions from which they are reasoning.

28. Kohlberg, "Stage and Sequence," p. 380.

It is worth adding that the meta-ethical character of subjectivist reasoning has also been neglected in empirical work formulated outside the Kohlberg framework. While subjectivist moral reasoning has long been recognizable in various empirical studies, it has generally been conflated with a wide variety of other phenomena so that conclusions about these broader phenomena—"alienation," "anomie," epistemological "relativism," "identity crisis" (or "confusion")—cannot be applied to subjectivism alone.

For example, in Kenneth Keniston's classic study of alienated youth,[29] a central finding was the "ideological distrust of ideology" on the part of the "alienated."[30] Their alienation, in his terms, was "unprogrammatic."[31] Alienated youth were typically engaged not only in questioning particular values but also in a meta-ethical questioning of the *possibility* of objective or valid moral judgment. For example, one subject reveals:

> I don't really believe what I write in this 'philosophy'—that is, I can't find any reason to believe it . . . any objective basis for accepting any set of values, any philosophy, etc., rather than any other.[32]

He continues, adopting an explicitly subjectivist position: "If I say 'should be' it is just my own personal emotional reaction to the question."[33] Keniston, in fact, found a general pattern of meta-ethical skepticism that was intimately connected with a more general epistemological skepticism:

> Their philosophies are solipsistic, emphasizing the subjective nature of truth and concluding in many cases that any philosophical commitment is quintessentially arbitrary.

29. Kenneth Keniston, *The Uncommitted: Alienated Youth in American Society* (New York: Delta Books, 1960).
30. Ibid., p. 192.
31. Ibid., p. 76.
32. Ibid., p. 62.
33. Ibid.

As a consequence, these youth conclude, "even human consensus about values seems impossible: when apparent consensus occurs, it is probably based on misunderstanding."[34]

Yet by "alienation" Keniston meant something far broader than subjectivism: alienation was meant to cover all those diverse phenomena that involve "an explicit rejection of the values and outlooks of American culture."[35] Such a rejection, whatever its basis, would be classified as alienation on this account:

> There is no *a priori* reason why the rejection of American society should entail any one set of supporting or associated beliefs. . . . Men have rejected their society for a variety of reasons: because they had some ideal future society in mind (as with youthful socialist and communist revolutionaries the world over); because they harked back to some earlier social order, often romanticized, which they sought to recreate in the present (as with reactionary revolutionaries); or at times because they held in higher regard some non-material kingdom of the spirit for which the "real world" was but an anticipation, a purgatory, or a preparation.[36]

Alienation, in Keniston's account, would cover all these phenomena. Even the unprogrammatic form of alienation that Keniston found in his interviews was not confined to subjectivist responses. Many of his alienated subjects advanced moral claims that they appeared to regard as valid and that purported to justify rejection of *both* the existing society and all positive alternatives to it. On these grounds their alienation was classified as unprogrammatic whether or not it also involved a rejection of moral claims as such.

The same point can also be made about other influential conceptualizations of alienation. Meaninglessness, normless-

34. Ibid., p. 193.
35. Ibid., p. 8.
36. Ibid., p. 76.

ness, anomie, and self-estrangement have all been defined so as to apply to psychological states that are likely to be accompanied by some rejection of the legitimacy of moral claims but that are also compatible, at least theoretically, with the acceptance of their legitimacy.[37]

The study of epistemological development, like the study of alienation, has conflated ethical subjectivism with other phenomena—when it has touched on it at all. This has proved to be the case even in the one empirical study devoted explicitly to the investigation of "relativism."[38] In Perry's extensive longitudinal study of Harvard undergraduates,[39] relativism was clearly interpreted as the *recognition* of multiple frames of reference rather than as any actual acceptance of their equal truth or validity. For example, Perry defines "relativism" as

> a plurality of points of view, interpretations, frames of reference, value systems and contingencies in which the structural properties of contexts and forms allow of various aspects of analysis, comparison and evaluation in multiplicity.[40]

It is true, of course, that relativism in this broader sense may thus coincide with subjectivism in our sense of the term involving a claim about the possibility of resolving normative questions.[41] For example, one student classified at a relativistic position (in Perry's sense) commented:

> I wasn't sure there was anything in particular to follow. I, you do begin to wonder on what basis you'd judge *any*

37. See, for example, Melvin Seeman, "On the Meaning of Alienation," *American Sociological Review* 24 (1959): 783–91; and Robert Merton, *Social Theory and Social Structure*, enlarged edition (New York: The Free Press, 1968), especially pp. 209–20.

38. Perry, *Forms of Intellectual and Ethical Development.*

39. Perry (p. 8) studied various groups of Harvard undergraduates including one sample of 109 students, 67 of whom provided protocols over a four-year period.

40. Perry, *Forms of Intellectual and Ethical Development*, "Glossary."

41. It might even be plausibly argued that relativism in Perry's sense is a necessary but not a sufficient condition for subjectivism in our sense.

decision at all, 'cause there really isn't—ah, . . . too much of an absolute you can rely on . . . or you can base an ethical system.[42]

Other relativistic students similarly remarked:

I'm sure there are things that I'm not questioning now that I should be. Whatever "should be" is . . .[43]

if you don't have some sort of standard outside of yourself, what is going to be your standard? And so I don't really have one, and admittedly I'm in a lot of difficult problems. . . .[44]

However, people may be relativistic in Perry's sense without making any meta-ethical claims at all—whether relativistic or objective—or while taking moral positions that are, in fact, clearly incompatible with subjectivism in our sense of the term. They may acknowledge multiple frames of reference but nevertheless commit themselves to one particular framework.[45] Furthermore, relativism in Perry's sense is a general epistemological position; it is not confined to ethics.

Just as subjectivism may be intimately related to the philosophical questioning investigated by Perry, it may be—but is not necessarily—intimately related to the searchingly personal questioning investigated by Erikson under the notion of "identity." For a meta-ethical position may form the crucial component of what Erikson calls the "ideological source of identity."[46] Any "historical era," we are told, "offers only a limited number of socially meaningful models for workable

42. Perry, *Forms of Intellectual and Ethical Development*, p. 116.
43. Ibid., p. 117.
44. Ibid., p. 130
45. Perry's relativism is a broader category than the relativism encountered in the Kohlberg literature, first, because it requires only recognition of multiple frames of reference (rather than a claim about their equal validity), and second, because it applies generally to forms of knowledge (rather than specifically to ethics).
46. Erik Erikson, *Identity: Youth and Crisis* (New York: Norton, 1968), p. 35.

combinations of identification fragments."[47] What we have called a subjectivist position may undermine an individual's identity options by undermining the ideologies available to him to justify those options. This connection between meta-ethical questioning and identity questioning is apparent in Erikson's portrait of Luther: "a young person in whom justification had become the core-problem: how to *know* when God justifies—and why."[48]

The same connection can be seen perhaps even more starkly in Perry's paraphrase of a number of his interviews:

> If all I have been taught up to now is open to question, especially to my question, then my sense of who is responsible shifts radically from outside to me. *But I see too that my questions and my answers are likewise open to question.* Yet if I am not to spend my life in questions about questions and am to act, choose, decide and live, on what basis am I to do it? I even see now that I have but one life to live.
>
> This, then, is the issue of individual personal commitment in a relative world [italics in original].[49]

Although identity questioning (or "confusion")[50] may be intimately connected to meta-ethical questioning in this way, the two are not always so closely related. Unpublished empirical findings by Podd, analyzed by Kohlberg and Gilligan, strongly supported the conclusion that "morally transitional subjects were in transition with regard to identity as well as morality"—but not the reverse.[51] In other words, Kohlberg and Gilligan concluded that identity questioning is a necessary but not a sufficient condition for the questioning of conventional morality, which, they hypothesize, must lead in turn either to

47. Ibid., p. 53.

48. Erik Erikson, *Young Man Luther: A Study in Psychoanalysis and History* (New York: Norton, 1958), p. 89.

49. Perry, *Forms of Intellectual and Ethical Development*, p. 34.

50. Erikson has replaced the earlier term *identity diffusion* with the term *identity confusion*. See Erikson, *Identity: Youth and Crisis*, p. 212.

51. Kohlberg and Gilligan, "The Adolescent as a Philosopher," p. 1078.

"transitional relativism" or to "transitional" movement to principled (stage 5 or 6) thinking.[52]

On this account, therefore, not only may subjects undergo identity questioning without becoming subjectivists (because they may, instead, move to Kohlberg's stage 5 or 6) but they may also undergo identity questioning without questioning conventional morality at all (because identity questioning is a necessary but not a sufficient condition for movements beyond stages 3 and 4). We thus encounter the same difficulty with the identity literature as with the other empirical classifications ("alienation", "anomie", epistemological "relativism") that appear related to subjectivism: because the proposed classification ("identity crisis" or "confusion") has been applied so as to conflate subjective and objective meta-ethical positions, it has no direct application to the problem of distinguishing the ideological conditions for the occurrence of the former from the ideological conditions for the occurrence of the latter.

While empirical studies of subjectivism—apart from the moral development research with which we began—thus appear to shed little light on the identification of the ideological conditions that support subjectivism in an individual belief system, certain clues to the character of those ideological conditions may be gleaned from the moral development literature itself. Consider, first, that the early analyses of subjectivism as regression included the claim that the new stage 2 reasoners differed from those ordinarily encountered not only in the fact that they understood stages 4 and 5 but also in the fact that their reasoning was "jazzed up with some philosophic and socio-political jargon."[53] A second clue is provided by the fact that the later analyses of subjectivism as a transitional 4 1/2 position made clear that subjectivism differed from other "disequilibriums" because it involved "questioning the validity of general

52. Ibid.
53. Kohlberg and Kramer, "Continuities and Discontinuities," p. 109.

moral terms."[54] By contrast, a state of disequilibrium in the ordinary sense occurs when "the inconsistencies of an existing stage are perceived."[55] Rather than merely questioning the inconsistencies in a given stage, subjectivists questioned the validity of moral terms *in general*—a questioning that, as noted above, they supported with "some philosophic and socio-political jargon." These two facts together indicate that much could be accomplished for the understanding of both the genesis and stabilization of subjectivism if the relation of meta-ethical skepticism ("questioning the validity of general moral terms") to other elements of a subject's belief system (the "philosophic and socio-political jargon") were clarified.

The need for this line of analysis, independent of the classifications provided by Kohlberg's six stages, is made clear by the fact that not only are nonmoral elements of an individual's belief system not included in the stage classifications, but variations in fundamental meta-ethical claims and assertions are explicitly omitted as well. Such questions have, instead, been relegated to the "purely metaphorical notion of a stage 7" in Kohlberg's theory.[56] Even his stage 6, we are told, cannot directly answer such questions as "Why be moral?" "Why live?"[57] "What good is justice?"[58] "Why be just, in a universe that is largely unjust?"[59] These are questions that are "left over" even at stage 6. To expect a moral stage in the cognitive developmental sense to deal with such ultimate questions, we are told, would be to place "excessive demands" on it.[60]

54. Kohlberg, "Continuities in Childhood and Adult Moral Development Revisited," p. 24.

55. Turiel, "Conflict and Transition," p. 8.

56. Kohlberg, "Continuities in Childhood and Adult Moral Development Revisited," p. 55.

57. Lawrence Kohlberg, "The Ethical Life, the Contemplative Life and Ultimate Religion—Notes toward Stage 7," Social Science 154 Lecture (December 1970), Mimeographed, Laboratory of Human Development, Harvard University, p. 4.

58. Kohlberg, "From Is to Ought," p. 217.

59. Kohlberg, "Continuities in Childhood and Adult Moral Development Revisited," p. 54.

60. Kohlberg, "The Ethical Life . . ., toward Stage 7," pp. 1–3.

Kohlberg's stages, in other words, deal with normative ethical principles for resolving problems of moral choice; those principles rest, in turn, on certain meta-ethical presuppositions that are not directly supported by the moral stages themselves but are relegated instead to the metaphorical notion of a stage 7. In this light, we might argue that subjectivists have proved to be problematical for the theory precisely because they question the meta-ethical assumptions presupposed by the moral stage classifications.

Kohlberg's own interpretation of subjectivism has consistently restricted it to what might be called its normative ethical variety. In light of one normative ethical position (that of the "universal principles" of stages 5 or 6), another normative ethical position (that of the conventional morality of stage 4) appears dubious. "Intense awareness of relativity," Kohlberg argues, "implies a search for, or a dim awareness of, universal principles in terms of which conventional morality seems arbitrary."[61]

This interpretation rests on the distinction between the "rules" of conventional morality and the "universal principles" of postconventional morality:

> By a moral principle we mean a mode of choosing which is universal, a rule of choosing which we want all people to adopt always in all situations. . . . There are exceptions to rules then but no exceptions to principles.[62]

He gives as examples of "rules" that may require exceptions the prohibition against stealing (which needs to be overridden to save a life in the Heinz dilemma) and the prohibition against killing (which needs to be overridden when the sacrifice of certain lives may be required for the saving of many more).[63] "Principles," by contrast, have unconditional validity compared with the more limited applicability of conventional morality:

61. Kohlberg, "From Is to Ought," p. 180.
62. Lawrence Kohlberg, "Education for Justice," in T. Sizer, ed., *Moral Education* (Cambridge, Mass.: Harvard University Press, 1970), pp. 69–70.
63. Ibid.

The claim of principled morality is that it defines the right for anyone in any situation. In contrast, conventional morality defines good behavior for a Democrat but not for a Republican, for an American but not for a Vietnamese, for a father but not for a son.[64]

It is in this sense that the rules applicable to a limited range of contingencies may seem arbitrary when compared with "principles"—"modes of choosing" which, it is thought, are universal in their validity and exceptionless in their application.

However, as we have seen, one may question rules and/or principles without necessarily accepting *other* universal principles as the basis for bringing them into question. There is no reason to believe that meta-ethical questioning *requires* a commitment to *any* particular normative principles, even to universal ones. Once possibilities of this kind are acknowledged, the need becomes apparent for the kind of exploration launched here into the rationales underlying subjectivism. Such an exploration, I argue here, supports a consistently meta-ethical interpretation of subjectivism, one that does not simply place it in the gaps between particular normative ethical stages.

64. Kohlberg, "From Is to Ought," p. 185.

Appendix B: Ambiguous Cases

The mere fact that the seven positions presented in chapter 2 constitute the only consistent combinations of the six premises defined there does not, by itself, guarantee that they would constitute viable empirical classifications. It is worth pausing for a moment to consider some of the ways in which subjects might escape classification into the proposed scheme.

The various possibilities are presented in chart 3. First, some reasoners may not think about meta-ethical issues at all (possibility A). Second, if they think about meta-ethical issues, they may make special ideological assumptions that render consistent some alternative position falling outside the scheme (possibility B2a). This may occur because the logical relations discussed earlier are modified by those assumptions (B2a1) or because entirely different assumptions are employed than those presupposed by the scheme (B2a2). Third, a reasoner may simply have an inconsistent position. He may realize this (B2b1) or he may be completely unaware of it (B2b2).

More interesting for our purposes are those reasoners who explicitly deal with meta-ethical issues but who cannot be classified uniquely at one of our proposed positions. Two such cases of a generally subjective kind are worth mentioning for illustration.

CHART 3

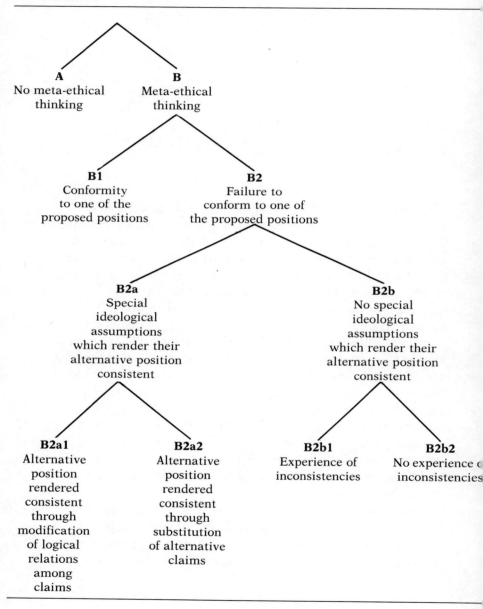

Nancy is a Yale College senior who plans to work for a year or two before going on to graduate school in clinical psychology. During the interview she vacillates between relativist and personalist views, and, at some points, subjective universalist views as well.

One example of her vacillation occurs over the question of condemning the druggist in the Heinz dilemma. "I don't know what his moral system was," she begins. "According to my system I think he'd be wrong; according to his, maybe he was following his ethical system—in that case he's right."

"If he was going along with his convictions," she says of the druggist's refusal to sell the drug, "then I guess he was right." Since she is willing to judge the druggist by *his* values rather than by her own, these responses suggest the relativist position.

Upon further reflection, however, she revises her conclusion:

> A. Let me think about this. I don't think I could judge him. I think I would have to know why, you know. It seems to me that he would be ethically wrong. But, you know, I'm not God and I can't go around saying what other people's values are.
> Q. Not saying what they are?
> A. Or should be. Why should I say what other people's values should be? I'm confused is what I am.

Nancy's hesitation about whether she can judge others continues in the dilemma about the efforts of a medieval city to deal with the Plague. By walling up a portion of the city—condemning those inside to certain death—the bulk of the population could be saved. The question arises whether Nancy would condemn the prince if he walled up the infected houses—not in order to save the most lives but rather to consolidate his position of power.

"I can't condemn him" is her first response. When pressed, she adds, "I told you, I can't judge him." But then she reconsiders: "Just let me say, I will condemn him, but it's not based on anything and I have no right to condemn him." "Or, my condemnation doesn't mean a thing," she adds. "Because that's my condemnation—it's based on my own feelings and values, whatever they are."

She has vacillated between saying: (a) that she "can't judge him" (what we have called a personalist position); (b) that she can judge him (presumably by her own values), "but it's not based on anything" (what we have called the subjective universalist position); and (c) (in the case of the druggist) that she should judge him in terms of *his* values (which would yield a variant of the relativist position).

To these various positions Nancy adds, at one point, a more bizarre view. In considering a physician's decision in a euthanasia case (dilemma 2, appendix D), she says that she can "think" someone is wrong but cannot "say" it. "I can't say he's wrong," she explains, "I still think he's wrong, but I certainly can't say it."

Since she is admittedly perplexed ("confused is what I am"), these vacillations from one position to another do not affect my general claim that every consistent and fully developed view on the six premises can be assigned one, and only one, position in the scheme.

None of her vacillations, furthermore, casts any doubt on whether she has adopted a generally subjective view of morality. Therefore, I include Nancy among our subjective reasoners even though there is little basis for deciding to *which* of the four subjectivist positions she belongs. As she says, looking back over her own tortuous reasoning, "I still have no objective values, no matter what way you want to phrase it."

Tom is a recent Yale graduate teaching secondary school. He shows a similar pattern of vacillation among our various subjective positions. In his response to the Heinz dilemma, he admits to confusion in attempting to judge others but eventually seems to arrive at the subjective universalist formula—that others "should act with regard to their consciences."

> A. If you asked the question, was he obligated to steal the drug, would anybody under those circumstances be ob-

ligated to steal the drug to save her life? I don't think, I don't think that's the case.

Q. Why's that? (long pause)

A. I suppose I basically believe each person has to decide what he's got to do for himself, so you can't say [he] "has a moral obligation to do" (pause) I don't know, it's very confusing when I start talking about Heinz. I can talk about myself I suppose better. I really, I'm not that clear on how other people should act. I guess I come down they should act with regard to their conscience and I could say what I would hope that they would do, but not what they, I don't feel safe in saying what they're obligated to do.

However, this position comes very close to relativism. For example, in the case of the druggist, the issue of classification (between subjective universalism and relativism) would turn on how Tom deals with the problem that his formula—each person deciding for himself—may yield conflicting judgments of the same act:

A. I mean people have to be able to be, are ultimately, responsible to themselves and not to the society or to the laws, or to what somebody else thinks. So that the druggist is ultimately responsible to what he really considers to be consistent with his conscience. And it might be what I'd, what I would consider to be worthless or useless or ridiculous.

Q. Or immoral?

A. Or what I would think would be immoral. But it wouldn't make it immoral for him. There's no absolute morality. Ultimately, I think it has to come down to each individual accepting responsibility deciding for themselves *(sic)*.

Here he seems to exemplify the form of subjective universalism, mentioned in section 4.5, that would closely parallel relativism in sanctioning judgment of each person by his own values—but all according to a single universalizable principle such as that each person should be judged according to his own (respective) conscience. He does not, however, hold to this position consistently and arrives at something closer to relativism when he considers social problems involving several actors. He begins to judge others *both* by their values and by his own, simultaneously offering conflicting judgments from differing "points of view." This becomes clear in the Plague dilemma:

> I guess you have to look at this from two points of view: whether it's moral from their point of view and what criteria I would use to judge that, and whether it was moral from my point of view, that is, whether I would consider it moral knowing what I know.

Judging it from his own point of view, he applies the criterion of "whether there was caring involved." In the plague situation, he says, "It seems as though they acted not out of caring for the people they walled up but out of fear for their own lives." Hence, he concludes, "From my point of view, it doesn't seem very moral."

But when conflicting motives become involved in the same policy, even those judgments restricted to Tom's own point of view become less manageable. For example, he is asked to judge the policy if the prince ordered it "out of compassion" but the soldiers acted "out of fear." "Then," Tom responds, "it would be moral for the prince and immoral for the soldiers. I don't think you can judge it apart from the intentions of the people involved."

Note that these judgments of intention (whether "caring" was involved) are applications of Tom's values—judgments from *his* own "point of view." In addition, Tom tries to judge the policy from the "point of view" of those involved, that is, according to *their* respective values.

"And from their point of view," he says, "if they were acting with regard to their conscience—which is to do what they felt was consistent with their values—then from their point of view it would be moral." On the other hand, "If they were acting disregarding any sort of values that they had, then it would be 'immoral.'"

Sometimes, then, Tom appears to take the relativist position of judging *both* from his own "point of view" (whether "caring" was involved) and from the "point of view" of others (whether they were "consistent" with their own respective values). At other times, however, he appears to apply a single principle to everyone (namely, that each person must decide conscientiously for himself). On such occasions his apparent relativism shades into the subjective universalist position of the same principle applied consistently to everyone (each person following his "conscience"). Occasionally, he also suggests a third position: that he cannot judge others at all, for they must decide for themselves. This last position would, of course, be personalism.

Like Nancy, he seems perplexed by a recurring issue facing the subjectivist positions: how can it be appropriate or defensible to apply one's admittedly subjective or arbitrary moral judgments to others who disagree? If I judge others by my values I seem to be imposing my arbitrary preferences on them. If I judge them merely by *their* values I undermine, or bring into question, the sense in which I can simultaneously affirm conflicting values of my own. Tom very nearly reached a kind of resolution to this problem by affirming as his own value that everyone should be judged only by their respective "consciences." But this position did not leave enough room for *other* values he wanted to affirm—in particular the value of "caring" for others, a value he would like to apply to everyone.

The root problem seems to be that once he judges others (such as the prince in the Plague dilemma) by the extent to which they "care" for others, he is judging them by a value that may differ from their *own* "conscientious" values. On the one hand, if he does not apply such values of his own to others, then he seems to take them less seriously as moral values. They lose the characteristic structure of morality since they are no longer prescriptions for how anyone should act under specificable conditions. On the other hand, if he does apply such values of his own to others, then he is taking the conscientious values of others less seriously, by imposing his values on them—even though he admits his own values to be arbitrary and subjective. If he really believes in "caring" as a value, then how can he refrain from applying it to others? Yet if he really believes each person should be judged only by the values of his *own* conscience, how can he impose a value such as caring on those who disagree?

In section 4.5 I explore subjective strategies for dealing with these issues. Here it is worth noting that Tom's vacillations, like Nancy's, do not offer a theoretical challenge to the scheme. My contention is that every consistent and fully defined position on the issues defined by the six claims will fit one, and only one, of the proposed seven positions. Tom escapes our classificatory net only by vacillating between positions and by being unsure of how to respond to some of the issues posed. But, as we saw in section 4.5, this is only because he is grappling conscientiously with a difficulty at the heart of all the subjectivist positions.

Appendix C: More on the Scheme of Ethical Positions

In Chapter 2 I noted that the six moral claims in the scheme of classification could be combined into only seven logically consistent positions. I defined the claims in such a way that two logical patterns apply:

    a. A moral position satisfying a given claim must, if it is to be consistent, satisfy all those *following* it in the hypothesized order.

    b. A moral position rejecting a given claim must, if it is to be consistent, reject all those *preceding* it in the hypothesized order.

These relations are assumed here, based on the definitions presented earlier. Consider the first pattern. If a position satisfies absolutism (claim 1), then it must also be inviolable (claim 2), objectively valid (claim 3), universalizable (claim 4), and apply to others (claim 5) as well as to onself (claim 6). Similar inferences can be drawn about inviolability (claim 2), yielding objective validity (claim 3), universalizability (claim 4), interpersonal judgment (claim 5), and judgment of self (claim 6). In general, conformity to a given claim requires conformity to those following it in order, but not to those preceding it.

Similarly, rejection of a given claim requires rejection of those preceding it. For example, rejection of claim 6, judgment of self, would require rejection of interpersonal judgment (claim 5), rejection of universalizability (claim 4), (since the position would then not apply consistently to everyone), rejection of claim 3, objective validity (since it could not then be justified in its consistent application to everyone), and rejection of claims 2 and 1 (since these two claims obviously include the objective validity claim). In general, rejection of any claim requires rejection of those preceding it; acceptance of any claim requires acceptance of those following it.

Consider one of these logical patterns for consistent positions—that acceptance of a given claim requires acceptance of those following it. This pattern alone is sufficient to reduce the consistent possibilities to the seven proposed here. Let us number the claims C1, C2, C3, etc.:

a. C1 is either + or −. If C1 is +, then by the hypothesized pattern, C2, C3, C4, C5, and C6 must also be +. Hence the pattern + + + + + + (position I).

b. If, on the other hand, C1 is −, then it may be followed by C2, which is either + or −. If C2 is +, then by the hypothesized pattern, C3, C4, C5, and C6 must also be +. Hence the pattern − + + + + + (position II).

c. If C2 is −, then it may be followed by C3, which is either + or −. If C3, is +, then C4, C5, and C6 must also be +. Hence the pattern − − + + + + (position III).

d. If C3 is −, then it may be followed by C4, which is either + or −. If C4 is +, then C5 and C6 must also be +. Hence the pattern − − − + + + (position IV).

e. If C4 is −, then it may be followed by C5, which is either + or −. If C5 is +, then C6 must also be +. Hence the pattern − − − − + + (position V).

f. If C5 is −, then C6 may be either + or −. If C6 is +, then the pattern − − − − − + (position VI) results.

g. Left over from steps b through f is the possibility that each − claim is followed only by other − claims. This yields the possibility of − − − − − − (position VII).

Hence this pattern of logical relations limits the consistent possibilities to the seven positions.

However, although these seven possibilities are collectively exhaustive of the consistent positions on these premises, as defined here, it must be emphasized that there are other possible ways in which ethical positions might be classified. In particular, it might be argued, this scheme classifies together positions that might usefully be subdivided. For some purposes, certain positions classified together in this scheme might be distinguished.

This can be seen if we separate the elements of the scheme into two dimensions. One dimension, which might be labeled epistemology, concerns the kind of justification or basis we have for making moral judgments. Whether or not moral judgments are rationally unquestionable and whether or not they are objectively valid in any weaker sense fall along this dimension. If we assume that they cannot be rationally unquestionable without *also* being objectively valid (the former being a stronger claim which includes the latter), then there are three consistent possibilities on these issues, as seen below:

Epistemology

	Rationally unquestionable	*Objectively valid*
(a)	+	+
(b)	−	+
(c)	−	−

The (a) position would assert that values are both rationally unquestionable and objectively valid. The (b) position rejects the claim that they are rationally unquestionable but asserts that they are objectively valid. The (c) position rejects both claims.

Let us now consider another dimension of claims about morality—a dimension that might be called the "scope" of moral judgments. Principles may be rigorous (that is, exceptionless universal laws), they may be universalizable,[1] they may permit interpersonal judgment,[2] and they may permit judgments of self.

I assume that the consistent possible positions on these issues are those set forth below. For convenience, I have numbered them from 1 to 5.

Scope

	Rigorous (or exceptionless) principles	Universal- izability	Inter- personal judgment	Judgment of self
(1)	+	+	+	+
(2)	−	+	+	+
(3)	−	−	+	+
(4)	−	−	−	+
(5)	−	−	−	−

These two dimensions can be combined to define the array of possibilities depicted in chart 4. I have indicated the positions from the scheme of seven positions with roman numerals. I have also indicated the clearly inconsistent possibilities with X's. These inconsistencies result directly from our definitions in chapter 2. They require, for example, that there cannot be objectively valid positions that are not also universalizable (or that do not permit interpersonal judgment or judgment of self)

1. Universalizable judgments need not be cast in the form of exceptionless principles. They may, for example, be weak, prima facie, or ceteris paribus. This distinction is discussed further in section 2.1.

2. There is the theoretical possibility, not explored here, of a commitment to judgment of others—but not of oneself. Such a reasoner, because he rejects judgment of self, would be classified as rejecting both *inter*personal judgment and judgment of self. He would, therefore, be categorized along with the amoralists (at position VII). Although this conflation would be misleading for certain purposes, it does not affect the argument here. It is also a bizarre possibility that I believe to be of interest only for classificatory purposes.

CHART 4

Scope					
Judgment of Self	+	+	+	+	−
Interpersonal Judgment	+	+	+	−	−
Universalizability	+	+	−	−	−
Rigorism	+	−	−	−	−

Epistemology

Rationally unquestion-able	Objectively valid		(1)	(2)	(3)	(4)	(5)
+	+	(a)	I	III	X	X	X
−	+	(b)	II	III	X	X	X
−	−	(c)	IV	IV	V	VI	VII

and that there cannot be positions that are rationally unquestionable that are not also universalizable.

Once these obviously untenable positions are eliminated (indicated by X's), nine alternatives remain. Positions I, II, V, VI, and VII are uniquely identified with one position in this scheme (possibilities a1, b1, c3, c4, and c5 respectively).

However, positions III and IV appear twice. This means that our scheme of seven positions would classify together possibilities such as c1 and c2 (at position IV) and a2 and b2 (at position III). The question for theory construction is whether at these two points the scheme of seven positions classifies together positions that need to be distinguished.

Possibility a1 refers to judgments that are rationally unquestionable but not cast in the form of exceptionless principles. If there are general principles at all, they would be weak or prima facie in form. The intuitionism of W. D. Ross offers an example of this position.[3] Like other forms of intuitionism it would be classified at position III in our scheme of seven positions. It is differentiable from the varieties of intuitionism encountered earlier, however, in that it lays claim to intuitions about particular cases that are beyond reasonable question.

Although this a2 possibility requires some dubious epistemological assumptions, it can be given a coherent construction. The question, for our purposes, is whether it is misleading to classify it at position III along with other versions of intuitionism. At least with respect to the arguments presented here, this conflation problem poses no difficulties: it does not affect either of my two claims about the scheme. First, the scheme classifies all consistent positions on the six premises at one, and only one, position in the scheme. Second, the scheme reveals the avoidability of the assumptions that produce subjectivism. For it reveals that position III (and in some cases position II) can be constructed to fall short of all the expectations but offer a coherent nonsubjectivist position nevertheless. Neither of these claims is affected by the fact that position III might be further subdivided in the way shown in chart 4.

The same response can be made to the other conflation, the one between c1 and c2. Position IV, as we have defined it, could be subdivided into a subjective universalism committed to principles that are *both* universal and exceptionless (so that they cannot be weak or prima facie). Although this distinction might be interesting for some classificatory purposes, it does not affect the arguments presented here.

3. See W. D. Ross, *The Right and the Good* (Oxford: Oxford University Press, 1930).

Appendix D: Moral Dilemmas

The first two dilemmas are standard Kohlberg dilemmas. The fourth was suggested to me by Marie Rogers. Dilemmas 5 and 6 were suggested to me by Bernard Williams and were adapted from his essay "A Critique of Utilitarianism," in J. J. C. Smart and Bernard Williams, *Utilitarianism: For and Against* (New York: Cambridge University Press, 1973), pp. 97–99. Variation 6b was suggested by one of the interview subjects during his response to 6a. All these dilemmas were posed with persistent probing about the rationales, if any, that a reasoner was able to offer for any substantive responses to the dilemmas.

1. In Europe a woman was near death from a special kind of cancer. There was one drug that the doctors thought might save her, a form of radium that a druggist in the same town had recently discovered. The drug was expensive to make, but the druggist was charging ten times what it cost him to make the drug. He paid $200 for the radium and charged $2,000 for a small dose of the drug. The sick woman's husband, Heinz, went to everyone he knew to borrow the money, but he could get together only about $1,000, which is half of what it cost. He told the druggist that his wife was dying and asked him to sell it at a lower price or let him pay later. But the druggist said, "No, I discovered the drug and I'm going to

make money from it." So Heinz got desperate and broke into the man's store to steal the drug for his wife.

    a. Should Heinz have done that? Was it actually wrong or right? Why?

    b. Is it a husband's duty to steal a drug for his wife if he can get it no other way? Would a good husband do it?

    c. Did the druggist have the right to charge that much when there was no law actually setting a limit to the price? Why?

[Answer d and e only if you think he should steal the drug.]

    d. If the husband does not feel very close or affectionate to his wife, should he still steal the drug?

    e. Suppose it wasn't Heinz's wife who was dying of cancer but Heinz's best friend. His friend didn't have any money and there was no one in the family willing to steal the drug. Should Heinz steal the drug for his friend in that case? Why?

2. The drug didn't work and there was no other treatment known to medicine that could save Heinz's wife, so the doctor knew that she had only about six months to live. She was in terrible pain, but she was so weak that a good dose of a painkiller like ether or morphine would make her die sooner. She was delirious and almost crazy with pain, and in her calm periods she would ask the doctor to give her enough ether to kill her. She said she couldn't stand the pain and was going to die in a few months anyway.

    a. Should the doctor do what she asks and give her the drug that will make her die? Why?

    b. When a pet animal is badly wounded and will die, it is killed to put it out of its pain. Does the same thing apply here? Why?

3. Heinz variation (addition to dilemma 1)

If you were the only person in town who was well enough acquainted with the druggist to know how to steal the drug, and a total stranger who was dying of the disease came and asked for your assistance in stealing it (assuming it could be obtained in time in no other way), would you be morally obligated to risk the penalties of the law and assist him?

What if you discovered, after looking into the background of the stranger, that he was an active self-proclaimed member of the Nazi party? Would that change the moral question in any significant way?

4. The Plague
During the Middle Ages a city in Italy managed to avoid the ravages of the plague by setting up a quarantine. However, since the officials had no knowledge of how the disease was transmitted, they decided that all those houses showing any evidence of the disease should be walled up and sealed off from any possible contact. As a result, a substantial number died, either from suffocation or starvation (including many who did not have symptoms of the disease at the time but lived with those who did). However, most of the citizens were saved and the city was the only one in the area to survive the plague intact.

Do you think there is any way that you can judge whether such a policy was morally justified in those circumstances?

(If uncertainty is expressed) What factors would be most important if you were the prince and you had to make the decision immediately—before the situation worsened?

5. There is a religious sect in Holland that strongly objects to the use of modern medical techniques. When one of their children is caught in a road accident, the parents try to prevent a doctor at the hospital from operating. Should the doctor go ahead since he has decided this is the only way to save the child's life? Or should the doctor refrain from operating out of respect for the dictates of their religion?

What if the patient dying were not a child but an adult member of the sect who objected himself to the operation (we're assuming that there is no time for legal action to resolve the problem, although the doctor may be threatened with the possibility of subsequent legal action)?

6. George is married, with a family, and has just gotten a Ph.D. in chemistry. The job market in his field, however, is very bad. He is finally offered a job, arranged by a friend of the family, in a company that does research in chemical and biological warfare. George objects to that kind of research, but his wife wants him to take the job because he would otherwise be unemployed. The friend of the family tells George that he wants him to take the job because if he doesn't, the company is likely to hire another candidate, a brilliant young chemist who may contribute some major breakthroughs to that kind of warfare (which the friend also objects to). What are the factors George should consider in coming to his decision? Is this a moral question? Is there any way other people can judge it?

7a. Jim happens to be taking a trip to South America. In the course of that trip he happens to pass through a small, remote village where Pedro is the local chief of police. Pedro has decided that he and his assistants are going to execute, for no apparent reason, 20 Indians who have been selected arbitrarily. They're about to carry this out when they realize that they have a foreign visitor in the village. To commemorate Jim's unexpected visit, Pedro offers him the following proposition: if Jim will agree to execute the first of the 20 Indians, Pedro promises to let the other 19 go free. Let us assume that Pedro is able, somehow, to demonstrate that he will keep his word, and let us assume, in addition, that the use of force to somehow prevent the execution of the 20 is out of the question. One may also consider the effect of Pedro's promising never to conduct such executions in the future. Is there any way that you can judge what Jim should do?

b. Consider the following variation: Jim is traveling through South America with his best friend, and Pedro promises that if Jim will execute his best friend (in place of the first Indian), he will let all 20 Indians go free.

Index